W9-BUP-756

# the
# emerging
# church

Bruce Larson and Ralph Osborne

Edited by Richard Engquist

# the
# emerging
# church

WORD
BOOKS ‖‖ Waco, Texas
*Publisher* London, England

*Authors' Dedication*

To the Lord of the Church
and all of His faithful people
who are helping Him to create
"the new thing" in our time.

# CONTENTS

When historians of the future look back at the 1970's, they will doubtless see this as an era of chaotic change in the Church, a day of new beginnings, and a strange mixture of despair and hope, frustration and boldness, disillusionment and expectancy.

Simply to read the chapter headings of books being written at this time is to note the confusion that marks the life of the Church today. For example, this is the day when the Church is . . .

"totally irrelevant";

"rediscovering its mission";

"as archaic as the furniture of our ecclesiastical past";

"alive and pregnant with the hope of tomorrow."

Depending on what voice you may listen to, the Church is at its worst, at its best, or in total mediocrity.

A recent letter from a brilliant and discerning friend castigates us for continuing to emphasize the Church in our time . . . and a second letter from an equally "aware" friend thanks us for our ministry within the framework of the institutional Church. Somewhere in this confusion of sound, the voice of God is speaking His authoritative word — and we must listen for His voice to guide and direct us in the days ahead.

This book is basically a report of what we have heard as we have sought to listen to that "still small voice" in the midst of the intense noise on every side. Over the past years, we have had the privilege of working with a great number of laymen of all ages and of both sexes, and with clergymen of most major denominations and all theological persuasions. We have traveled widely and listened long to these churchmen representing virtually every shade on the theological and ecclesiastical spectrum. This has provided a unique opportunity for us to become acquainted with the hopes, needs, and heart-deep feelings which will color the Church of the '70's.

9

We hear a sound of hope, a calling forth of a newly emerging Church, a demand for priority and commitment, and a word of instruction as to what the Church is to be. That voice among the voices says little to us about structure, institutional form, and traditional patterns. It speaks rather of new goals, considerable resources, and fresh strategies for the 1970's.

At the outset, therefore, let us express our hope that this book will self-destruct within ten years! Whatever new vision of God we may discern in the '70's will be outmoded by the '80's. Whatever new strategy is adequate to meet the challenge of the Church today will be of little value for the Church day after tomorrow. Whatever new forms are freshly given for the Church now a-borning will be an institutional albatross for the Church of a decade hence. We must not worship the new simply because it is new. Neither can we keep our eyes on the past simply out of respect for tradition.

This introduces a key word which will be highlighted again and again in this book: the conjunction "and." Whereas the heady polarities of our day seek to divide us into an either-or camp, the mark of the emerging Church will be its emphasis on both-and. For generations we have divided ourselves into camps: Protestants and Roman Catholics, high church and low, clergy and laity, social activists and personal pietists, liberals and conservatives, sacred and secular, institutional and underground.

The emerging Church will not choose up sides in such a fashion. Rather, it will affirm what is valuable in each emphasis, bringing together the most helpful of the old and the best of the new, blending the dynamic of a personal Gospel with the compassion of social concern. The Church of the '70's will find its ministry being expressed by a whole people, wherein the distinction between clergy and laity will be that of function, not of status or hierarchical division. In the emerging Church, due emphasis will be placed on both theological rootage and contemporary experience, on celebration in worship and involvement in social concerns, on faith and feeling, reason and prayer, conversion and continuity, the personal and the conceptual. The word "and" will be an often-used conjunction in the emerging Church.

We are not talking, therefore, about *renewal*. Renewal is a concept foreign to the emerging Church. Renewal implies that the Church was once what God intended it to be and that our task is to bring back that golden age. From its earliest beginnings until now, the Church has been in the process of becoming, and it shall always be so. If the Church is true to its Lord, it may never properly say that it has "emerged." In both the past and the present, the Church is in a process, moving toward a fulfillment of its calling. We have nothing of perfection to which we may return; we have no golden age to which our deepest longings draw us; we have no plumbline from the past which is adequate for the Church of the future. Not *renewal* but *a new thing* is our concern as we begin to witness God's fulfillment of His own word spoken through the prophet Isaiah: "Remember not the former things, nor consider the things of old. Behold, I am doing a new thing; now it springs forth, do you not perceive it?" (Isaiah 43:19).

That "new thing" must find its own authentic form, life-style, and purpose, whether in a small group meeting in a home, a remote rural church, a beleaguered inner-city congregation, or a great cathedral parish. Wherever there are a few individuals willing and ready to be Christ's people in their own situation and place, there the emerging Church is coming into its own. "Do you not perceive it?"

# PART I
# DEFINING GOALS

# Chapter 1 ||| INADEQUATE GOALS

Not long ago we were meeting with a businessman in his office and it surprised us that, though the telephone rang intermittently, he made no effort to pick it up. Finally one of us asked how he could resist answering the phone.

"It is there for my convenience — not to tyrannize me," he replied. "I could never do my job properly if I gave in to the demands of the telephone. If it's important for someone to get in touch with me, he knows he can write for an appointment."

Very few of us have discovered this kind of freedom or got our priorities in order to the point where we are no longer victimized by peremptory demands on our time and attention.

The principle of the squeaking wheel is very much in operation today in our society. Whoever complains the loudest tends to capture our attention. In a family it is the difficult child who demands and gets the lion's share of the parents' time and energy. In the business world, the American Management Association cautions firms not to build their staffs around the weakest members, lest efficiency be sacrificed in catering to them. Within a church, care and concern are often lavished on "problem" officials and parishioners who are most vocal in expressing their own needs.

The squeaking wheel principle is also obvious in society at large. Among the thousands who are working to effect changes in some of our established structures and institutions, the ones who get the most attention and publicity are those whose voices are most strident, whose ideas and methods are most extreme. At the governmental level, little is heard about those officials who work quietly behind the scenes to bring about necessary change, bind up a nation's wounds, and "bring us together" as a people. Rather, those officials who use their offices as a platform to stir up passions and drive the populace into armed camps too often win a wide audience and occupy a prominent place in our newspapers and television broadcasts.

The squeaking wheel gets the oil. But sadly, this can lead to a squandering of energy and resources if the result is simply that we put band-aids on festering sores or skip about from one clamorous problem to another.

What has all this to do with the need for adequate goals in the emerging Church? Simply this: the squeaking wheel principle is just as prominently in operation within our churches as anywhere else.

Every clergyman soon discovers that the Church has the amazing capability of providing more problems than there is time to deal with them. We both found this early in our ministries and subsequent years have only strengthened us in this conviction.

In a typical parish, the choir is invariably short of tenors, or some irritation has resulted from poor congregational attendance at the latest cantata. The women's association nominating committee never seems to find the right persons for all the available jobs. The church school is perenially short of good teachers, and most of the classroom furnishings would not be acceptable in a second-rate public school system. Funds are always in short supply. And dear Mrs. So-and-so is forever able to communicate effectively that "the pastor has not called on me lately."

There is no shortage of problems. An entire career can be maintained solely at the problem level, with the pastor no more than an ordained mechanic racing from problem to problem with his little bag of ecclesiastical tools. In those brief periods when all of the machinery seems to be meshing smoothly, he frantically catches his breath and waits for an S.O.S. call from the next disaster area. If your goal for ministry is being able to handle problems efficiently, you are scarcely describing the concept of ministry portrayed in the Book of Acts!

Within a problem-centered ministry it is rare to find that worthwhile goals are being set and met. To put it bluntly, goal-setting is something of a lost art in our churches, as in our families and even in our lives as individuals.

Have you taken the time to determine whether you are pursuing goals which are wrong, inadequate, or outmoded? Recently we did this in an effort to pinpoint false goals that have misguided us and some of the churches we have known and served. You can see our conclusions in the chart on the next page. As an exercise in self-discovery, it's not bad. You may wish to try something similar in terms of your own situation. Be as honest with yourself as you can be.

Years ago, some friends of ours set for themselves the dual goals of a large income and a home in which there would be a game room for the children and their friends. Both parents had been brought up in families with small incomes and with small houses. There was never enough money, even for necessities, nor was there an attractive place to which friends could be brought and entertained. These "depression memories" color the thinking and determine the actions of the "over forty" set more than we care to admit.

Eventually, in the case of our friends, these goals were achieved: a lovely home and money in the bank. But additional factors had been at work which had not been anticipated. The four children seemed to appreciate neither the house nor the

| | Wrong Goals | Inadequate Goals | Outmoded Goals |
|---|---|---|---|
| Personal: | A large income. Comfortable home with game room for the kids. | To be an adequate person always. Not to hurt anyone.[3] | Early retirement. Security. |
| Family: | Always to be loving.[1] Family altar.[2] | College education for the kids. Well-behaved children.[4] | Close-knit family.[5] No arguments. |
| Church: | Increasing membership. Larger budget. | Efficiency. New building program. | Great preaching. A faithful "calling program." |

1. A wrong goal because I'm kidding myself.
2. Why is this *really* so important to me?
3. Wishy-washy. Where there is love, there is always some hurt.
4. For my sake or theirs?
5. A close-knit family is fine, but what about the children's independence and need to rebel?

money. And for one of the four a sorry ending to the story was written in a gloomy, dark-panelled juvenile courtroom when he was convicted of larceny and possession of narcotics. On the surface, the parents' goals looked good. But they were dead wrong.

Some of our goals are not necessarily wrong but simply inadequate. For example, none of us wants to be a failure. We want to be adequate persons in every situation: adequate parents, adequate spouses, adequate churchmen, adequate in our professions. To be adequate — what an inadequate goal!

Speaking personally, as we review the past we see with gratitude that God has made good use of our experiences and training. However, He consistently seems to be able to use our mistakes, failures, and even our sins to contribute to our growth more effectively than any of those things in which we have proved our adequacy.

A friend of ours is the pastor of a large, unusually vital congregation in which there is a mutual attitude of appreciation and support between pastor and people. It was not always so. Not long ago, the rumblings of discontent in the official boards of that church were ominous. The pastor simply must go!

The boards were summoned to meet together; a catalogue of the pastor's failings and failures had been outlined in some detail. The time had come to make official what had been thoroughly discussed in telephone conversations and in "special board meetings" of which the pastor was not advised. The hour of confrontation had arrived.

After a rather awkward opening prayer, our friend quietly acknowledged that he was well aware of the reason for the meeting. He told the board members that he appreciated and respected their concern for the church and admitted honestly that he had failed to be an adequate pastor or leader. Then he went on to share with them some of his own feelings and fears, his sense of inadequacy and his frustrations. This was no psychological gimmick. It was simply a man giving himself to his co-workers in a vulnerable, costly way.

When he had finished, there was a long silence. Then one of the board members acknowledged that he had failed his pastor by not being a teammate in ministry with him. This opened the floodgates and one after another expressed openly his personal frustrations and failures. The catalogue of the pastor's failings was forgotten. They all discovered one another in a new and profound way.

Forgiveness was asked on all sides. Prayers for one another were said. And a new birth was given to a congregation, its official boards, and its pastor.

The unity and power of a dynamic fellowship that came to that church were not made possible by adequate clergy leadership. They were the fruits of inadequacy faced up to, shared vulnerably, and transformed by the amazing workings of God's kind of love. A goal of adequacy would have resulted in nothing like the new spirit of fellowship that now marks that congregation.

There are some goals which are neither wrong nor inadequate, but outmoded. They are no longer worthy of our time and attention.

Someone we know had as his primary goal early retirement from his job. He looked forward to doing the things he thought he so much wanted to do. He worked hard, watched his pension account grow, and finally reached the point of retirement.

Now he does not have to get to the office, nor does he have reports to complete. He has no more business decisions to make. There is plenty of time — but he doesn't know how to use it. His wife's harried words the other day were: "I married him for better or for worse — but not for lunch!"

Even such an innocent appearing goal as a pension plan can become a devastating problem. Many clergymen we have known have reached their mid-fifties with real questions about how to spend the last decade of their active professional life. They are tired of trying to be all things to all men. They are disillusioned with church politics, with feelings too easily hurt, with the pettiness that is no less obvious among "God's people" than among any group of human beings. They long to pitch the whole business and move out — like Abraham — toward a new land of hope and promise. Perhaps they could better serve Christ if they were laymen!

But then these weary servants of God begin to examine the alternatives. What vocation can you begin at age fifty-five? How can you provide for a family during a retraining process? And ten years hence, how can you retire if you give up your ministerial pension (which you must do if you leave the ranks of the clergy)?

If a man's primary goals are somehow tied to financial security, his decision has already been made for him. He'll stay where he is, putting aside his Abrahamic dreams and waiting out ten long, tedious, unproductive years until the church honors his "long years of fruitful service" with one final ham and green bean dinner.

Then it's too late. When a man's dreams have died, the man himself has died in part. And his retirement merely commemorates a kind of death that occurred long before. It is no longer adequate — if indeed it ever was — to aim one's life toward a pasture at the end of a long road.

Too often we labor away with goals that shackle and inhibit, rather than free and excite us. This is true of our personal and professional lives and of our "institutional" lives as well. It is painfully true of the Church. Those of us who are part of the Body of Christ in its various institutional forms can be led by goals which are totally wrong, quite inadequate, or no longer relevant for the emerging Church.

Almost without exception, "successful" churches and pastorates are measured in terms of their giving records and rates of membership growth. If the statistical summary indicates growth, there is a vital church! If it indicates decline, there must be something wrong with the pastor! In spite of official disclaimers that numbers and amounts are inadequate criteria of meaningful ministry, every denomination requires its local churches to submit an annual report which basically has to do with "how much" and "how many"; seldom anything else. The obvious implication is that increasing numbers and a swelling budget are the primary goals of the local church.

Recently a presbytery (a Presbyterian area-unit of church government) on the East Coast became concerned about the declining statistics reported by its churches. An experimental task force has now been created to work with a pilot grouping of congregations for the express purpose of stemming the statistical ebb-tide. The fact that such emergency measures have never before been taken *for any other area* of the churches' concern underscores how crucial numbers are in the definition of that presbytery's goals and objectives.

Another presbytery we know of recently spent a long, wearying day dealing with many items on a crowded docket. One matter to be acted upon was a committee's recommendation that a certain pastor of another denomination be enrolled as a member of the presbytery. He wished to change from one denomination to another for personal reasons which seemed perfectly legitimate.

All the members of the presbytery supported the committee's recommendation; everyone wanted the man to be enrolled. But well over an hour was spent in discussion — not of "whether" but of "how." Motions submitted from the floor were followed by amendments and substitute motions and even a "privileged motion." Voice votes were so close at times that standing votes were necessary. Finally, the matter was taken care of and business could proceed.

Only then could the last item on the docket be presented: a report by the presbytery's committee on evangelism. By now it was after 10 P.M., long past the hour for adjournment, and everyone was bone-weary.

The report proved to be quite unusual. There were no dull statistics, no mimeographed data. Instead, the committee had invited three men from another part of the state to tell what was happening in their congregation: the pastor, a key layman, and a young staff member working with the youth of the community. What they had to say was exciting. Things were happening in their parish: lives were being changed, young people were sharing a ministry with the oldsters, men and women were becoming deeply involved in personal and corporate ministries all over the place. These were "New Testament people" with good news to share.

But the hard pews, the tiring discussions on procedure, and the late hour had taken their toll. Exciting news fell on dull ears and saturated minds. Twenty minutes later, after three men had tried their best to bring a word of hope about the Church, the machinery ground to a halt and the presbytery was adjourned for another month.

Again, the matter of goals had been the hidden item on the agenda. Apparently, a primary goal for that presbytery was that things be done "decently and in order." The excitement of God's new thing in the Church today was secondary to that. Order had taken precedence over ardor.

No one questions the necessity for orderly procedure. Confusion is no certain mark of the Kingdom. But order in itself is an inadequate goal for the Church. An excellent strategy, perhaps, but an inadequate goal.

The last three decades have marked the busiest period of construction in the history of the Church. Wherever we go we are struck by the sheer quantity of new construction and major rebuilding projects undertaken since the end of World War II. All things being equal, the Church of the '70's should be housed in physical facilities superior to that of any previous generation.

Isn't it strange that this very period of physical prowess in the life of the Church is apparently also a period of spiritual impotence? Is this juxtaposition merely a coincidence, or does it say something very basic about our priorities?

Just as we can report on the proliferation of building projects, we must also observe from personal experience that not much of permanent value seems to be happening within a good number of those magnificent buildings. Much too often we have sensed a "business as usual" quality to church life.

A clear-cut example of this phenomenon is seen in the conventional occasion of worship. Most congregations seem to expect very little to happen when the people of God assemble for praise. The mimeographed "order of worship" is just like that of the previous week. The straight-in-line pews and the raised pulpit imply that spectators are to gather for an event which will be led by (or is "performed by" more accurate?) a professional whose place is not *with us* in the pews.

The music (grand, somber, or sentimental), the "prayer-language" reserved for this place alone, and the almost total lack of spontaneity provide little sense of celebration of a people in whom dwells the resurrected Christ!

If a congregation has set as a primary goal the building of a place fit for the worship of Almighty God, it will find disillusionment when the project is completed. Unless something has happened to the people, the place is not very important. Once again, the project may be worthy but as a goal it is inadequate. Erecting a new building may be the right strategy for a congregation, but it is never an adequate goal.

Our generation has also experienced a subtle shift which even yet is not well comprehended. Formerly, a pastor and a congregation might rightfully have as an objective a great preaching ministry. The descriptive word "pulpiteer" was once apt for the expounders of God's word. And this had a certain validity. The pastor was often *the* educated person of the parish. He could read, write, and communicate his knowledge to a less educated flock. "The wise shepherd and the dumb sheep" was not an inaccurate image, and the sermon was valid not only for its Christian content but in a rudimentary sense for its educational value.

One of the major changes in the church scene over the last forty years is in education, not for the pastor but for most church members. Now the preacher communicates with people who are as well or better educated than he. From the pulpit on a Sunday morning he faces a congregation liberally sprinkled with B.A.'s, M.S.'s, and Ph.D.'s. What is more, virtually everyone in the pews — regardless of the extent of his formal education — has a sophistication and broad general knowledge undreamed of a generation ago, created by the explosion in the field of mass communications.

In this context, "getting across" to the people is quite a different matter from the case of a generation ago, and serves a different purpose. Great preaching, in a historic sense, is no longer a proper goal for either people or pastor. At one time, perhaps, but no longer.

Last year a well-known church in the Midwest scheduled a series of special services featuring the greatest preachers of our day. A sensitive person might have wept to read the publicity releases for that series, for *every one of the guest preachers was retired from the active pastorate.* It was more a nostalgic memorial service than a dynamic means of ministry for present needs.

True, the emerging Church will require great sermons, but great sermons for the '70's will find a more contemporary means of communication than that employed by yesterday's pulpit orators. Whatever form preaching will take, that form will not in itself be a goal for the emerging Church. A right strategy, yes, but not a goal.

The question of facing up to wrong goals is not simply a matter of correcting poor business procedures. The Church can always survive inept performance. Rather, when our goals are wrong, inadequate, or outmoded, what we do in attaining those ill-conceived goals leaves us unfulfilled. We give them our best effort, the goals are accomplished, but nothing ultimate has been achieved. We are restless with something unfinished and we don't quite know why. What we sought to do we have done — and things are not very different from before.

We believe that it is possible to find a radically different approach.

# Chapter 2 ||| AUTHENTIC GOALS

Is it possible to drift aimlessly through life without ever establishing goals or trying to meet them?

Not really. Whether we think about them consciously, or operate with vague notions and a half-hearted commitment, every one of us has both immediate goals (to get through college; to get a better job; to get married) and long-term goals (to be "successful"; to be "happy"; to get along with everyone). It is our goals, conscious or unconscious, which largely determine what direction our lives take, and whether we find freedom and fulfillment as individuals and as members of the human family.

Even if we never think in terms of specific goals at all, within us there is a whole constellation of "oughts" and "shoulds" that shapes our destiny by determining our behavior and reactions. Part of our problem is that each of us has goals that we had no part ourselves in establishing.

Many of these are unknown to us; most of them are not deliberately chosen. The example of our parents, the influence of friends or relations, books we have read, a "hero" type from our childhood or adolescence — all of these and many other factors operate unseen and unbidden to make us the kinds of people we

are and determine most of our significant accomplishments. This
is illustrated clearly in the case of one of us, who was influenced
in far-reaching ways by two seminary professors.

> One of those professors was a very special friend to me, and
> he shaped part of my goals for ministry. It wasn't anything spe-
> cific that I learned in his classes, nor an image of ministry that
> he proclaimed verbally which captured my imagination. Rather,
> it was the man himself. In my eyes he was an ideal pastor. As
> time went on, I began to see that a good deal of what I was doing
> in the local pastorate was simply a projection of what I thought
> he might do. His image — his way of doing things — made an
> indelible impression that resulted in a series of goals, and these
> goals shaped my ministry for a good long while.
>
> The other professor's influence was less profound and far-
> reaching, but in a peculiar way it provides an example of the
> subtle power we have over one another.
>
> This man was a very amusing person. He was challenging,
> yet he had an unusual style about him which stimulated my "in-
> ner goal-setting machinery" and wove its way into the substance
> of my being.
>
> Years later, while teaching a Bible study course, I found my-
> self standing one day in a peculiar — even a bit uncomfortable
> — posture. It occurred to me that I was standing in precisely the
> way that my theological professor would stand at times when he
> was at his best, lecturing us on the profundities of the Christian
> faith!

Unfortunately, these hidden factors that determine some of
our goals and behavior patterns are neither beneficial nor harm-
less. For example, this is how one of us describes his experience
as a family man:

> I don't know where I picked up my concept of what a Chris-
> tian family should look like, but I do know that that image (or
> goal) hampered my family for a considerable period of time.
>
> A goal I had set was that I would always remain in calm con-
> trol of every situation. This control was not to be a matter of

domination, but something given to me by my wife and children because they recognized my leadership and gladly teamed with me in a ministry as a united family.

My children would be attractive, obedient, open to gentle correction. Together we would demonstrate a life of prayer, with Christian fellowship, little tension, and a readiness to pitch in and help one another as needs arose.

This was my idea of what a Christian family looked like, and where it came from I don't know. But for a long time I labored under considerable guilt because this was *not* the image my family projected.

To be truthful, my family and I have never found prayer together to be a very meaningful experience. Usually we have had family prayers when I felt guilty enough to insist that we sit down and have a devotional time together. When the children were young, this was fairly easy to arrange, but as they grew older I had to force the issue to have this nice, religious experience.

It was frustrating for me, it was meaningless for my children, and my wife was caught in the middle: wanting to help me do the thing I thought we ought to do, yet conscious that this was not a maximum experience for the children.

What a relief it was finally to discover that a Christian family does not necessarily have to have family devotions. This was a freeing realization for me and enabled me to establish new goals that had more to do with freedom than with religious behavior.

Somewhere along the line I had also picked up a picture of what marriage should be like. It involved a lot of romance combined with a sense of teamwork; sort of a marching-hand-in-hand-into-the-sunset kind of image.

This vision or goal I had for marriage simply didn't allow for the kind of snits I found myself getting into. It didn't provide for the loss of communication with my spouse which became so pronounced that a lot of hard work was required to bridge it. It didn't even permit idiosyncrasies to exist in our particular relationship.

Again, what a freeing experience it was to see that a wrong set of goals had given me a wrong image of what married life was all about.

What we are trying to indicate is that there is a process by which we can deliberately set our goals: goals that are right for us in our particular situations, which may be totally unlike anyone else's. Our goals should be uniquely ours. If they happen to agree with those of our neighbors, it is by a blessed coincidence, not a careful design.

Therefore, let us begin at the beginning and talk about our personal lives, our family life, and our vocation, whatever that may be. What are we really aiming at? What are the primary targets that will determine for us what we are going to do? Without referring to anything you have read or heard or seen in someone else, what would you most like to see happen in your own life? What would you most like to see produced in the life of your family? What are you aiming at in terms of your vocation? This is what goal-setting is all about.

If you sat down with a blank piece of paper and a pencil and tried to answer the questions indicated above, you might have a bit of a problem because the subject is so broad. At least in ideal terms, we have an almost limitless choice of goals. Perhaps, therefore, we need to get a clearer picture of some of the things God may have in mind for us from which we can then define our goals.

In our search for ultimate purpose — the kind that over-arches all lesser objectives — let us look to Jesus Christ Himself for guidance. Referring to His own principal goal, He said, "I have come in order that they might have life, life in all its fulness" (John 10:10, TEV). In other words, what God intends for all His people is an expansive kind of life; a life of great value; Life with a capital L. What does such a life consist of?

Both the gospels and the epistles put a great stress on freedom, culminating in that great cry of Paul, "Freedom is what we have — Christ has set us free! Stand, then, as free men..." (Galatians 5:1, TEV). The abundant life is a life of freedom.

Neither of these terms, Jesus' "life" nor Paul's "freedom," is a vague generalization. They are not wistful hopes, nor fuzzy abstractions. They have to do with specific relationships that make up what we call "the Kingdom of God." Let us take a look at these right relationships in four specific areas.

*One's Relationship to God.* At the very heart of the Christian faith is the question of man's relationship to God. This is a primary emphasis of the New Testament and of the vast bulk of all religious writing. Wrong relationships to God run the gamut from complete indifference to casual lack of concern to mistrust to fear to resentment to hatred.

Through Jesus Christ, however, we are introduced to an entirely new relationship which can only be described as personal, warm, exciting, and even enjoyable. The Westminster "divines," thinking in terms of both man's goals and his relationship to God, asked (in the Shorter Catechism): "What is the chief end of man?" Their answer: "The chief end of man is to glorify God and to enjoy Him forever."

In some ways we have been able to glorify God, although perhaps we do this better corporately than individually. But we would have to say that we don't know a great deal about enjoying God. Nevertheless, this is one mark of a right relationship with Him.

If the Shorter Catechism is correct, God's ultimate goal for us as regards our relationship with Him is both *glorification* and *sheer enjoyment.*

The authors of this book began their individual adventures with Christ with a sense of tremendous gratitude to God for His love and forgiveness. After a life thoroughly sprinkled with failure, compromise, and self-condemnation, the assurance that "God does indeed love *me*" and that the past was forgiven was good news indeed.

That initial gratitude for God's forgiveness was complicated, however, by later and repeated wrongdoing, wrong-thinking, and wrong-desiring. Even though we had been forgiven, neither of us was much changed. For one of us, the result was a redoubled effort to proclaim God's Word. For the other, it meant the hiding of failure and an inner disquiet and self-loathing. Our spoken words and outward actions glorified God and, indeed, even helped others to honor Him — but neither of us found much enjoyment in the Almighty!

Only in later years did we discover that God's continuing love *indeed continued,* in spite of our individual failures. God's love was not dependent on our faithfulness, effectiveness, or goodness. That discovery meant that we no longer had to cover our failures with fanatic zeal nor hide them with aching despair. God knows us thoroughly — and still He loves us.

As we began to relax in that amazing relationship with God which His love makes possible through Jesus Christ, God became not only our Lord to adore and honor, to praise and obey, but our Creator-Friend to love and enjoy. Even more recently, we are beginning to sense something of God's enjoyment in His relationship to His creation.

How basic to the true meaning of love — accepting, honoring, serving, *and enjoying.* This describes a right relationship with God: a worthy goal for any man.

*One's Relationship to Himself.* Ours is a day of increasing self-hatred. Society itself seems bent on its own destruction. We pollute our atmosphere, soil, and water more recklessly every day, despite widespread knowledge of the consequences. Those who propose steps to halt the downward spiral are voices crying in the wilderness. Short shrift is given to plans and projects designed to preserve natural and human resources. Rampant selfishness at all levels of society hastens the day when the human race will have accomplished its own extinction. Is this not the ultimate in selfishness, which is rooted in self-hatred on a truly colossal scale?

Nowhere is self-hatred more obvious than in our great cities. The casual acceptance of physical and moral filth; the grab for power and influence and public funds (regardless of the real needs of the public); the pessimistic attitude that dooms every significant effort to alleviate social ills; the polarization of ethnic and racial groups; all these are indications not of man's struggle to survive but of his urge for annihilation.

A key figure in the mayor's office of a major midwestern city said recently, "I am convinced that there is a poison of self-hate in the bloodstream of the American city which is destroying the life of the inner city. Anyone who has an answer to that kind of self-hatred has the answer to the real problem of the American city today."

Most of us need look no further than our mirrors to discover the truth of these assertions. We don't like what we are, so we spend vast sums of money to alter our appearance and squeeze ourselves into a more acceptable form. We have become masters of the art of self-loathing.

Is there a solution to the problem of self-hatred?

Yes!

The good news of the New Testament has precisely to do with the fact that God loves us. We may be a mess; we may not look like much; our behavior may be far from ideal; but the amazing message of God's Word is that there is a love affair going on between the Creator and His creation.

When this news finally gets through to me in Jesus Christ, I am caught with the simple observation that if God loves me this much, there must be something in me that is lovable. One of the major effects of the transforming life of Jesus Christ is that He has set me free to love myself.

If I make this discovery, something happens which changes my attitude not only toward other people but to the very environment in which I live. I am worthwhile; other people are worthwhile; my physical surroundings are worth salvaging; the universe itself is beautiful and majestic.

On the surface, this form of self-affirmation may smack of egotism and self-aggrandizement. But, not so! So many of us have such little sense of self-worth that we are not giving much when we give ourselves to God in an act of commitment. It costs nothing to give a nobody to the Almighty!

But in Jesus Christ we experience the good news that we are of immense value to God. The Cross of His Son is the measure of that value. When we accept His measure of our worth, we have a real self to give Him — and the commitment of a valued self has meaning indeed.

In this sense, a valid and humble prayer would be, "Father, I thank you for your gift of *me* which you have made worthy through the loving sacrifice of Jesus Christ, and the self you have given I give back to you with gratitude. Use me, Lord; use even me!"

*One's Relationship to the Significant Others in His Life.* Needless to say, real life does not consist only of a relationship with God and with one's self. A love affair with God is splendid; a healthy love for one's self is a revelation. But there are individuals in the world besides ourselves, and some of these will not be ignored. We are married to them, we have given birth to them, we work with them, we socialize with them. We may relate badly to the "significant others" in our lives, but we cannot make them go away!

A wrong relationship with these significant others often takes the form of *manipulation.*

It does not take many years of married life for a perceptive husband or wife to discover how to manipulate his spouse into a desired attitude or action. Dropping a word of calculated praise or criticism; digging up an old bone of contention; preparing a favorite dinner; developing a headache at a crucial moment; dredging up past mistakes and shortcomings; wearing a certain dress or perfume; bringing up a subject guaranteed to strike sparks — these and many other ploys are all too familiar to veterans of the war between the sexes.

It is a simpler matter to manipulate one's children, for they are under our influence from the beginning of their lives. One father confesses ruefully: "Even before our second child was born, I knew how to manipulate my offspring. As time passed I found I could get them to do almost anything I wanted them to do. With one of them, for example, if I said not to do a certain thing, she would certainly do it!

"Our first system of allowances was started in this way. The children would be rewarded with the specified allowance if their behavior was good, if the garbage was taken care of, if their room was cleaned. The allowance was a means of manipulation.

"We learned quickly that we could give love or withhold it, offer praise or condemnation, not for the well-being of the child but simply to manipulate him into doing the things we wanted or being the kind of person we wanted him to be. But this destroys personal freedom."

Manipulation in business and in government is the rule rather than the exception. Anyone who has ever held a job or a political office knows how individuals can be played against each other, superiors "wrapped around one's finger," fellow employees and subordinates made to look responsible for one's own failures.

God's love enables us to relate to the significant others in our lives without manipulating them. Instead, Christ suggests His own pattern for such relationships — the pattern of personal vulnerability and affirmation.

Listen to the experience of one man:

> For much too long a time, I tried to maintain a certain friendship by always attempting to be adequate in the other person's eyes. He didn't know my feelings nor my failure because I was afraid this kind of honesty would cause a break in the relationship. I guess you could say I was manipulating him into friendship by pretending to be what I was not.
>
> I remember the first time I was really honest with him. I had begun a basic honesty with Jesus Christ. Being totally honest now seemed more important to me than maintaining a false friendship. So with some fear I shared with my friend what I was really like inside. I told him something about my lusts, hungers, fears, and failings.
>
> It would not have surprised me if he had condemned me or

broken our relationship. Instead of being rejected, I was accepted by my friend because the kind of person I was inside was the
kind of person he was, too! Honesty begets honesty. Together
we found each other in a deeper, more meaningful way.

This kind of transformation is possible between friends,
within families, among co-workers, and in churches. It is possible, in slightly different ways, between groups of people. To
suggest that it is also possible at national and international levels
is not within our area of competence. But does not world peace
wait for the time when nations find the freedom and grace to
acknowledge their mistakes, confess their failures, and ask the
forgiveness of world opinion?

Some years ago, a friend of ours was present at a most unusual meeting in India, attended by diplomatic representatives
of a number of Asian countries whose normally cordial relations
with the United States had been deteriorating. The American
representative, who had called the meeting, found himself faced
on all sides by suspicion and distrust. But instead of trying to
justify the policy of the United States, he began by acknowledg-
ing the many diplomatic mistakes that had been made, then went
on to outline new policies. As a result of this acknowledgment
of failure, the character of the meeting changed from one of hos-
tility to one of openness and cordiality.

Anyone can put this principle into practice in his everyday
life. To be vulnerable and affirming is part of the goal of freedom Jesus Christ makes possible in our relationship to the significant others with whom we live and work.

*One's Relationship to the World.* How easy it is to assume
that we need not concern ourselves with those outside the circle
of our immediate involvement. We can choose to ignore those
who live on the other side of town, or those who are of a different ethnic or cultural group. If we live in insular suburban communities, we can close our eyes to all the problems of the inner
city, along with the people who live there. It is easier still to

forget about the hunger and poverty, disease and filth, ignorance and superstition that exist in remote parts of the world. Or, if we do not choose to ignore these people and their needs completely, we can serve our self-esteem by "helping" in a rather detached way: writing a monthly check to support some nameless, faceless orphan in a far corner of the earth.

Once again, the example of Jesus Christ begins to change the direction of our attitude toward the world. Christ has become personally involved with me, with my daily life, my personal needs, my places of fear, loneliness, and brokenness. As He begins His transforming work in me, He gives me eyes to see the world in a new and different light so that I am no longer able to ignore it or to buy it off with the simple expedient of cold charity.

Now I begin to require of myself a costly involvement with the people of the world — and that world begins in my immediate neighborhood. The testimony of a man we know is a case in point:

"When I first got involved in the racial conflict in my community — in those days we called it the Civil Rights struggle — it was because I thought 'those people' needed my help. But the more deeply I became involved with those who had suffered injustice over the years, a strange change took place inside me. I began to feel some of the pain they must have been feeling. The despair and suffering that were a normal part of their existence became a part of my own.

"My involvement with them was beginning to be much more for my sake than for theirs. In order for me to be a whole person, I needed to lay my life down with these particular people in this particular community because I could not be whole without them."

In the Church, we are beginning to learn that the world does not need us as much as we need the world; *that is why Christ sends us into it.* His example is before us. We are disciples of Him who fed the hungry, healed the sick, and drove the money changers from the temple. Again, the freedom to be involved in the world's needs in a costly way is part of the Christian's life goal.

It may be possible to sum up these four right relationships by expressing them in a simple diagram.

### The Kingdom of Right Relationships

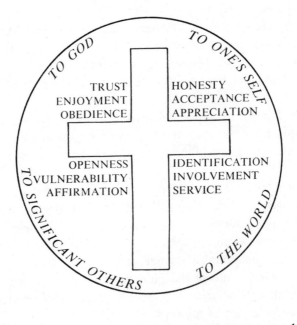

With this as a background, let's see what we can do about determining specific goals for ourselves, our families, and our churches.

*Personal goals.* In a small group of trusted friends, or with one intimate friend with whom you can be totally honest, raise the question of what you are really after in life. It may be necessary to break through some pretensions and preconceptions by asking questions such as these:

1. If I knew I had only five years to live, what would I most

want to have accomplished during that period of time?

2. If I knew I could not fail, if I had no family responsibilities, and if income were not an issue, what would I most like to try in the next three years?

Thinking through personal goals can be an eye-opening experience. It may reveal that we are too materialistic — or that we are not materialistic enough (if, for example, we are failing to provide adequately for our family). It may convict us of over-optimism or over-pessimism. It may revive a dream of long ago which is now capable of fulfillment. It may change the course of our entire life.

A friend of ours, a well-known aerospace engineer, is at this moment in a painful process of examining his goals and setting new ones. For years he has been deeply involved in studying the feasibility of a new, sophisticated missile system, pouring out his talents in researching a system that might one day add to the military capabilities of the United States. The almost-insurmountable problems he has encountered along the way have goaded him into maximum performance.

But now the situation has changed. The research has been completed and our friend knows that the system is in fact possible. He now has been asked to head up a group of men to move from research into design and possible production.

As we sat in his living room the other night, our friend raised questions about his personal and vocational goals. His comfortable home and way of life; the security of his more than adequate income — were these primary goals for him? As for his vocation, was it sufficient for him to be a masterful technician, a solver of complex problems? Now that it was possible to move from the realm of research to actual production of a system of destruction, what should he do?

Most of us never face such awesome questions. But every one of us needs the kind of friends who can help us to think and pray through what we are doing with the gift of life and to find, in fellowship, God's goals for us.

*Family Goals.* Has the time come for you and your spouse
to take a day away from the family with only one item on the
docket: to talk through the whole matter of adequate goals for
your marriage?

This kind of exercise cannot be done under the ordinary pressures of family life. Goal-setting for couples cannot be squeezed
in among the other priorities demanding your attention. Time
must be provided within a relaxed and comfortable setting. Then,
perhaps, the two of you can ask these kinds of questions:

1. What do I expect out of marriage that I could not have
if I lived alone? (Each of you make your own list.)

2. To obtain these goals, what changes would I like to see
in my spouse's characteristics, attitudes, and behavior?

3. To meet these objectives, what changes are required in
my own character, attitudes, and behavior?

4. What help or hindrance are our children in attaining
these goals?

5. When the children have left home and I have reached the
point of retirement, what would I most like to have accomplished
in life?

If we are at all honest with ourselves, we must admit how
impossible it is to be totally objective about one's spouse. Even
in a simple exercise such as the above, objectivity is very difficult
to achieve. Therefore, after grappling with these questions, it
may be helpful to invite one or two other couples in for an evening to lay before them the questions you have been asking and
the answers that you have begun to come up with. Share with
your friends not only the process of goal-setting, but some of
your feelings which that process evoked. See what these trusted
friends will say about the goals you are setting: are they worthy
goals for your marriage? In the process, you may help others to
set some goals of their own.

A second laboratory experiment in goal-setting is described
by a man who tried it only a few days ago:

All four of our bewildering offspring were at home and I raised these questions: What are we really after as far as our family is concerned? What goals are we operating by, intentionally or unintentionally? What should our goals be?

In the discussion that followed, these were some of the things that emerged. One son said bluntly, "We don't have goals as a family." Another son contributed, "Each of us has his own thing that's most important to him." "All we have are the six different goals of six different people," observed our daughter, "and they never quite mesh."

Then I asked, "But how do we really see each other?"

This led to a general pooling of ideas in which each one was encouraged to say how he viewed the other members of the family. With the exception of the youngest child — who found it all boring — everyone did so enthusiastically.

Where were family goals in all this? They weren't obvious at first. But the discussion did give us an opportunity to talk about who we were as individuals, which probably would never have happened if we had aimed for it. And as we talked about who we were, we began to see two family goals which none of us had been able to articulate before. The children saw them first:

1. Other people and their needs are of primary importance in determining family priorities and actions.

2. Each member of this family is encouraged to express himself in his uniqueness. Self-expression is highly valued!

After this long, occasionally hilarious, and very helpful discussion around the dinner table, I sat back and took a long look at these newly-seen goals. Frankly, I have mixed feelings about them. God isn't even mentioned in our family goal definitions, and that bothers me. Yet this is a fairly accurate outline of what really determines who we are, what we say, and what we do. And somehow I don't think God is disappointed at all.

We learned something else: this kind of conversation is not easy for us. We are not accustomed to thinking in these terms. Moreover, my wife and I found it hard to hear some of the implied (as well as spoken) criticism of the way our family has been run over the years. Nevertheless, we ended by asking ourselves, "Why did we wait this long to have this kind of conversation with our family?"

Perhaps some of the following questions would be "pump-primers" for a similar discussion around your table:

1. If my family were everything I want it to be, how would I describe it in single words or brief phrases?

2. (For the children) Before I leave home, what would I most like to see my family attempt or accomplish?

3. (For the children) If I were setting up my own home right now, what attitudes, customs, special activities would I like to see retained or reproduced in my new family? What present family attitudes and activities would I not want to repeat?

4. (For the parents) What would I most like each of my children to be, to do, or to accomplish by the time he leaves home?

5. (For the children) Before I leave home, what would I most like to see Mom and Dad learn, do, or be?

6. (For everyone) What attitude, trait, quality, or behavior pattern in me needs most to be changed? What do I think the others in the family would like to see changed in me?

7. What is the most frustrating thing about being part of this family?

8. What is the most enjoyable or satisfying thing in being a part of this family?

*Church Goals.* The same kind of process described above could be used within a church to help it find adequate goals. What are we really after in the church? What do we want to happen to the people of our congregation? What do we want them to look like, act like, and be after they have been part of the life of this fellowship?

A colleague of ours once asked an official of the Westinghouse Corporation how Westinghouse would run the church if it had that opportunity. The answer that came back was profound in its simplicity. "We would ask only two questions: *What product are we trying to produce? Are we producing it?"*

These two questions ought to be asked of every congregation and every ruling board of every church in the land. *What is your church trying to produce? Are you producing it?*

Again, these are not questions that can be dealt with by an individual, but only by a group of people within the life of a congregation who can work through the process of goal-setting together. Later on in this book (Chapter 9), some specific helps will be given to guide you in determining adequate goals for your particular church. At this point, let us give some thought to how this procedure might be initiated.

One church has an annual retreat for its officers, and the whole question of goals for the coming year is discussed. These church leaders look over the goals that were set the year before, and an evaluation of their performance is made. Then a new set of goals is determined for the coming year.

Another church holds a series of congregational retreats where the whole membership is invited to propose long and short-term goals. As these are gradually hammered out over a two-day period, they are "finalized" by the governing board of the congregation, then mimeographed and sent to all the groups, organizations, and activities of the church so that each of these units may measure its performance in terms of the particular goals.

We have recently heard of a certain presbytery which is in the process of setting new goals. This presbytery has had its fill of well-ordered meetings, tedious dockets, and complicated structures. The erosion of years had reduced the presbytery to the status of administrative machinery — a far cry from the supportive, discerning fellowship of peers ruling the church in love as the church fathers intended. It was decided that tinkering with the machinery would not be adequate. Radical restructuring was needed.

And these keen churchmen are settling for no less. A six-month moratorium has been declared on presbytery business other than that absolutely required by church law. During this period, all program committees of presbytery have been disbanded.

A three-day conference was held to share concerns, set objectives, and discern mission goals. This dynamic process continues as the representatives of the forty churches of presbytery gather monthly. At each meeting, the clergy and laity meet in groups of eight. Each group wrestles with the problem of turning concerns into goals, and reports to the presbytery as a whole. The meetings are held in a large hall with the small groups meeting around the room, thus enabling these churchmen to come to know one another personally and deeply as co-workers in God's Kingdom. Members of the presbytery have elected a group of pastors and laymen to lead them in this restructuring process on the basis of primary objectives and goals in mission.

All of the above presupposes that no church has ever been totally what God intended it to be. Further, it assumes that a successful program for last year might not be an adequate kind of church life this year under this year's goals. The definition of our goals should determine our emphasis and program. As goals change, everything the church does should be altered accordingly.

But before we can determine how to accomplish these goals we set for ourselves, whether personal goals, goals for our families, or goals for our churches, we had better take into account the resources available to us.

# PART II

# DISCOVERING RESOURCES

# Chapter 3

# SECONDARY RESOURCES

Remember the mad tea party scene from *Alice in Wonderland?* The March Hare is concerned because his watch has stopped. He shakes it, opens it up, and dashes in some butter. Still it doesn't work. "I told you butter wouldn't help it," the Mad Hatter comments wisely. "But it was the *best grade* butter," the March Hare replies wistfully.

This story speaks to all of us who have been trying to accomplish worthy goals by using the wrong resources. The best butter in the world won't make a broken watch run, and even the most excellent resources a church may possess won't help that church to meet its goals if the resources are inappropriate. Just as a church needs to find a proper set of goals, it also needs to discover (or rediscover) its true resources.

Our observation is that the Church is not using wrong resources so much as majoring in the minors. It has seized on valuable but secondary resources and inflated them in importance to the point that primary resources are all but forgotten.

For a moment, let yourself indulge in a bit of fantasy. Imagine that you have been given the responsibility of restructuring a local church from the ground up. You have been complaining about the church and your complaints have been heard.

Recognizing that you have wisdom and ability, as well as a real dedication to the church, the governing board comes to you and says: "We understand your concern for the church and we trust you. We'll scrap everything we are doing in terms of building, program, ministry, and services. Now you take us from the very beginning and we will rebuild the church just as you suggest."

What would you say to an opportunity such as that? What goals would you set, and what resources would you employ in order to meet them?

Some months ago, one of us had the opportunity to speak at the very first Sunday morning worship service of a new congregation. Not only was the congregation new, but so was the community in which it was located. There was no old tradition that had to be maintained. There were no carry-overs of inadequate programming that had to be continued. The congregation had the privilege of making a fresh start — a completely new beginning.

What a disappointment that morning provided! The service was as uncreative and traditional as any conventional service in any established congregation. The mimeographed bulletin looked like a hundred others. The chairs were lined up in rigid rows. A most inadequate organist was playing a most inadequate organ. A choir had been assembled for the occasion, but there had not been time to find the right voices, the right music, or even the right notes. One thing followed another with rigidity and lack of imagination. Instead of making a fresh beginning, the congregation simply carried over into a new context everything that individual members had learned from previous experiences.

Now, if you will, return to the fantasy situation suggested earlier and imagine with us that you have the opportunity to build a congregation from the ground up. The responsibility of goal-setting and utilizing right resources is yours.

One obvious move would be to gather a group of laymen who had the skills necessary to think through what this new church of yours is to be: for example, a banker to help with finances; a school administrator to outline a total educational program; public school teachers to assist with details for a church school; men and women with a variety of business skills to help with organizational structure.

You will also want trained musicians to plan a music program for the congregation; people with a broad knowledge of literature to set up a church library; sociologists and social workers to establish "missions of mercy"; perhaps experts in the field of rehabilitation for alcoholics and drug addicts; not to mention psychologists, psychiatrists and marriage counselors.

In a short time it will be necessary to consider constructing a new building to house this congregation of yours. Therefore you need the services of community planners to determine where the focal point of the community is likely to be in years to come. There must be room not only for the initial building, but also for expansion. And, of course, plenty of parking space.

With the location of the building determined, new questions arise: what kind of building? how large? how to be financed? More and more secular skills become necessary. Architects and contractors are followed in short order by subcontractors, builders, landscape artists, interior decorators, and all kinds of tradesmen and artisans. A financial campaign must be mounted (with professional consultants of the highest order) and the best stewardship material must be developed.

Ultimately the building plans are under way, and an adequate budget is assured. Now you need the right kind of leadership and the right kind of program. A pastor must be sought to lead this new flock. But no ordinary man will do. Only an outstanding preacher may fill this new pulpit. Not only must he be a brilliant preacher, but a likeable, warmhearted and warmhanded, enthusiastic, sympathetic leader of men. After all, it is he who will draw new people into this church of your envisioning.

And now the program! Obviously, a church school is necessary, as are a variety of activities for people of all ages. Sensitive

programming is essential to educate and involve the people of
the congregation. Curricula, specialized ministries, and recreational activities must all be instituted with great care and the most
modern techniques. Dynamic leaders must be enlisted to share
responsibility for the various groups that will make up a vital
church in your community.

Finally everything is in place. The beautiful building has
been completed, an excellent preacher is in the pulpit, lay leadership is giving its best, a program is available to meet the needs
of people of all ages, and the congregation is beginning to make
itself known in the community. The church you have dreamed
about is now at work.

This caricature — obvious as it is — has all too much in common with what many of us think of as a great church. It illustrates not only a popular, conventional image of the successful
congregation, but also one of the reasons for the intense criticism
of the Church in America today. If all we have to work with is
the familiar mixture of goals and resources in our caricatured
illustration, then the best we can do is simply juggle them into
slightly different arrangements. We may use a little more of this
and a little less of that, but if no other ingredients are available,
the net result will not be much different from what we already
know and work with.

What, exactly, is wrong with the congregation we have fan-
tasized? Taken one by one, the various components seem worthy
and sound enough. Surely there is nothing inherently evil about
utilizing secular skills and material resources in building a church.
Surely there is virtue in having fine preaching and well-planned
programs.

True enough. The trouble is that these conventional images
of the ideal congregation are so firmly entrenched in our thinking that we never consider the alternatives — which are endless.

Again for purposes of illustration, let us take a look at the
various characteristics of our imaginary parish and suggest one
or two possibilities as alternatives for each.

*Size.* What is the ideal size of a congregation? 5,000? 500? Well, why not fifty — or a dozen — or even five? In setting goals for a church or in attempting to discover and utilize its true resources, the numbers game can be devastating. Jesus said, "Where two or three are gathered together in my name, there am I . . . ." As we face the future and seek to find the shape of the emerging Church, let us bear in mind that quantity does not guarantee quality.

*Location.* Who says that the best place for a congregation is at the focal point of a community? Perhaps it should be hidden in a corner somewhere, at the heartbeat of where its members live and work and socialize. It is entirely possible that they will find themselves becoming a "community" in a deeper, richer way if they meet in a shopping center or school or community hall — or even in a private home. A "sanctuary" need not always be on spacious suburban acreage surrounded by a private parking lot.

*Building.* The passion to erect beautiful, expensive buildings is not a phenomenon unique to our generation. But it is more widespread now than ever before. So many pastors think they are falling down on the job if they are not constantly involved in building ever bigger and better houses of worship, educational wings, parish houses, recreational centers, and the like!

Consider the possibility that a church should own no property at all. For public worship, the members might rent a hall or a theatre or a high school gymnasium. Instead of pouring their available funds into a church building or school, an alternative might be to buy abandoned houses in a deteriorating neighborhood, repair them, and sell them at low cost to people who would otherwise never be able to own their own homes. (Some established churches in Elkhart, Indiana, have tried just such a project.)

It may be right for a particular congregation to have not a house of worship but a hotel, restaurant, or coffee shop to fulfill its unique goals for ministry. Real estate is, at best, a secondary resource and must not be given a primary role.

*Leadership.* For most of us, the dichotomy between clergy and laity is deeply ingrained in our thinking. Some of our most faithful church members find it impossible to conceive of themselves as full-time apostles. Rather, they think in terms of "following" and "supporting" a pastor — who, of course, has answers for the problems of the day and the clear responsibility of providing leadership.

Perhaps a particular church should not have a full-time pastor at all. Consider the possibility of calling a team of ordained clergymen, each holding a "secular" job during the week. The alternatives for pastoral leadership are endless.

Moreover, the idea that each layman must contribute leadership in the area in which he is a supposed "expert" can be deadly. If the businessmen within a congregation are expected to confine their leadership to business matters, they may never discover spiritual gifts with which God has bestowed them.

This is not to imply that it is wrong to exploit natural abilities and training. It is to suggest that a parish that operates like a well-oiled machine, with a highly-skilled professional staff and with a corps of laymen each fitting into his carefully defined niche, may be a congregation that looks outwardly successful but is indeed of little use in advancing Christ's Kingdom on earth.

In the above illustrations, all of the resources to which we have referred are secondary resources. They are good, but they are not the basics upon which the Church is to be built. Charismatic preaching, lay skills and talents, building and budget, creative curriculum, sensitive programming, participation of membership in attendance and stewardship — all of these may be important, but they have very little in common with the resources that seem to have had such a powerful effect on the Church described in the Book of Acts. The apostolic Church had little by way of the resources listed above. Their resources seem to have been different not only in *quantity* but also in *kind*.

# Chapter 4

# PRIMARY
# RESOURCES

The unsophisticated Church described in the Book of Acts took into account two basic resources which are largely ignored by the Church today. These two resources have to do with *divinity* and *humanity*. Unless these two basic resources are at work in the life of the emerging Church, we will be unable to fulfill our calling as the Body of Christ in our time, whatever additional resources may be available to us that were not available two thousand years ago.

The first of the two primary resources that God has given us for our ministry is *Himself*. It is crucial that we understand both the fact of God's continuing presence and the implications of that awesome fact.

In the New Testament, this word picture is drawn for us: "I am the vine, you are the branches. Whoever remains in me, and I in him, will bear much fruit; for you can do nothing without me" (John 15:5, TEV). The use of this metaphor is hardly accidental. Jesus employed imagery that was certain to be understood by His followers — the grapevine was an integral part of their daily lives. The relationship of the vine and its branches is one of function and interdependence; just so is the relationship between the living Christ and His people. The implication of the resurrection is that He *presently* lives. Where? *In His people,* say the Gospels.

Another striking analogy is found in Jesus' parable of the final judgment "when the Son of Man comes as king." All of the earth's peoples are gathered before Him, "the sheep" on one side and "the goats" on the other. And these are the king's astounding words: "Whenever you did this [showed mercy] for one of the least important of these brothers of mine, you did it for me!" (Matthew 25:40, TEV). The point is very clear: God not only dwells *with* His people, but *in* them. To assist one of the least of His people is to serve Him, not in a symbolic way but in actual performance of ministry to the King of kings.

Paul put this into a theological framework: "I have been put to death with Christ on his cross, so that it is no longer I who live, but it is Christ who lives in me" (Galatians 2:19-20, TEV).

"For you have died, and your life is hidden with Christ in God. Your real life is Christ . . . . This is the new man which God, its creator, is constantly renewing in his own image, to bring you to a full knowledge of himself" (Colossians 3:3-4, 10, TEV).

"When anyone is joined to Christ he is a new being: the old is gone, the new has come" (II Corinthians 5:17, TEV).

With examples like these and many others to guide us, we come to the conclusion that the obvious primary resource for the Church is Christ alive in His people. The emerging Church will take this fact as basic to its life and ministry. Let us note some of its implications:

1. When the Church gathers for worship, the living Christ being present among and within them, participation by the whole people of God is essential.

In the churches with which we are familiar, it appears that the basic resources for worship are the homiletic brilliance of the preacher and the musical talents of trained instrumentalists and singers. Congregational participation in worship is usually limited to ritualistic responses, such as a vaguely worded prayer of confession, a responsive reading from the Old Testament, or the

Lord's prayer. Little or no opportunity is provided for Christ present to have His say through His people. Indeed, we make sure that no opportunity for spontaneity is provided, lest it result in an undignified demonstration.

This is, of course, not always the case. Some months ago, one of us was invited to preach in a church in the western part of the United States. The host pastor made it clear that he wanted the sermon to last no more than eighteen minutes. When, after eighteen minutes(!), the sermon ended, the pastor immediately went to the lectern and asked the congregation to arrange their folding chairs in groups of four throughout the sanctuary.

After this had been done, the pastor posed two questions for discussion, based on the sermon and on his knowledge of the congregation. For the next twenty minutes, the "sermon" continued in that room. The discussion was free, spontaneous, and enthusiastic. People visiting the church for the first time found themselves involved in meaningful conversation with old-timers.

"I felt this morning as if I *belonged,*" someone remarked at the conclusion of the service — and this seemed to be the prevailing sentiment.

What the pastor had done was simply to take seriously the fact that the living Christ dwelt among His people. There were things that He wanted to be said. There was wisdom that He wanted to make available to His people that could not be accomplished solely through the words of the preacher. This experiment in sermonic dialogue let Him speak in many different ways through His very different people.

In another congregation, this one in the Midwest, it has long been the custom for laymen to lead in prayers. These men and women do not get up in the pulpit, but remain in the pews with their families. The impression given is that the prayers are truly those of the people of God at worship.

Unfortunately, it is a human tendency to take even free and spontaneous expressions of worship and quickly make them hidebound and predictable. As an illustration, take the case of a congregation which has a ministry to jazz musicians. Because these men work at night and sleep during the day, a special vespers service was scheduled, in which the musicians and their families could participate along with their pastor.

At first this jazz vespers service was exciting and open to spontaneous expression. The music — often unrehearsed — seemed to be a natural expression of worship and communication. An electric feeling of joyful celebration flowed through the congregation.

Soon the word got around that something exciting was happening at this church at six o'clock on Sunday evening. Their curiosity aroused, people came as spectators. Before long it became apparent that the participating musicians were now *performing*. A mimeographed order of worship was made up and distributed. There were the same conventional responses found in any traditional church worship service. The only distinctive thing about the sermon was that it was laced with words and phrases from the special vocabulary of the world of jazz. The music was good enough, but the spontaneity was gone, and with it the exuberant worship of God and the sense of communication that marks a family.

The same thing can happen easily to any innovation in worship. According to the words of a hymn popular among young people, "You gotta move when the Spirit says move." Instead, our tendency is to move when we are told to do so by the schedule on a printed bulletin.

2. If Christ dwells in His people, then the matter of administration might well be in the hands of laymen rather than the professional clergy. What happens too often is that the paid staff of a congregation is expected to handle administrative policy and details, and the church board — made up of laymen — usually serves only to approve decisions already made. Then, at congregational business meetings (all too often attended by only a small fraction of the membership) the actions of the board are approved in the same perfunctory way.

The result is that most of the members of the parish are far removed from the determination of policy which affects the entire church. Surely this is not the best alternative! Unless the church is run like a corporation, it must become possible for interested members to have a real part in administrative planning and program development. The Quakers have something to teach the rest of us in this area. In that tradition there is a "waiting for the sense of the meeting," accepting as fact that Christ is truly present among His people, moving them in the direction He has in mind for their community.

Sharp discussion may be essential; adequate research is certainly important; and the best knowledge available needs to be brought to bear on the church's business. But then there should be the "awaiting" on an awareness of Christ's presence and will, as matters are dealt with which need decisions. A time of silence is as important to a business meeting as is a period of discussion. It is our firm conviction based on years of experience in various groups and churches that Christ will always make Himself and His will known to His people through one another.

3. Another responsibility of a worshiping fellowship is to help individuals within the fellowship to discover their spiritual gifts,* which are equipment for the various ministries of the people of God.

---

* Spiritual gifts (*charismata* in the Greek) are referred to by Paul in his letters to the churches in Rome and Corinth and in his correspondence with his young disciple Timothy. From these letters, we can list at least these as spiritual gifts:

1. *Eternal life in union with Christ Jesus* (Romans 6:23). It is important here to remember that eternal life is not a future state but a present condition in which the other spiritual gifts are equipment for ministry.
2. *Preaching God's message,* from Romans 12:6 and I Corinthians 12:10.
3. *Serving others,* from Romans 12:7. Note that this is a gift, not a chore!
4. *Teaching,* from Romans 12:7.
5. *Encouraging others,* Romans 12:8. Are you an affirmer and a "spiritual cheerleader"?
6. *Sharing "what he has with others . . . generously,"* from Romans 12:8. Notice that it is a gift to be free to give.
7. *Authority,* Romans 12:8. On what basis does your congregation choose those who are to exercise authority? By popular election? Or by discerning who has been given this particular gift?

In churches today, officers and administrators are more likely
to exploit the talents of the congregation than to help them find
their spiritual gifts. Imagine what is going on in the minds of
church leaders when new members are received into the congregation. The superintendent of the church school sees potential
teachers and Bible study leaders. The church treasurer and the
chairman of the board of trustees may see new pledge possibilities and additional income for meeting the church budget. Even
the pastor may be blinded to the gifts that God is providing in
the form of individuals, and he may see only a statistical increase
in membership that can be reported with satisfaction to the
denomination in the annual report.

And so it goes. The leader of the couples' club, the president
of the women's group, the chairman of the men's organization,
the choir director — all see individuals and talents that may be
exploited, rather than persons to whom God has entrusted spiritual gifts that are to be discerned.

The emerging Church will do much more in terms of helping
people to discover and develop such spiritual gifts. The Church
of the Saviour in Washington, D.C., provides an example of how
this can be done. There, as the people gather for worship, a
definite attempt is made to help individuals discern their gifts,
find their calling, and receive direction from the Spirit of God.
An individual member may report awareness of what God may

---

8. *Showing of "kindness to others . . . cheerfully,"* from Romans 12:8.
9. *Wisdom,* I Corinthians 12:8.
10. *Knowledge,* I Corinthians 12:8.
11. *Faith,* I Corinthians 12:9. Faith is not something we do. We can only
appropriate it as a gift.
12. *Power to heal,* I Corinthians 12:9.
13. *Power to work miracles,* I Corinthians 12:10.
14. *Ability to tell the difference between gifts that come from the Spirit and
those that do not,* I Corinthians 12:10.
15. *Ability to speak with strange sounds,* I Corinthians 12:10.
16. *Ability to explain what these sounds mean,* I Corinthians 12:10.

There is no indication that Paul has hereby catalogued the spiritual gifts de-
finitively. There are perhaps as endless a variety of gifts as there are needs of
equipment for ministry and mission. The Holy Spirit has never been out of
stock nor out of date.

be saying to him — what he senses God wants him to do. The congregation listens in love and concern, provides encouragement and correction, and helps the person to see more clearly what God's orders may be. Some of them may respond to his vision and see in it God's orders for them.

Action in that congregation is not derived from a board decision which imposes a program or ministry on the church membership. Rather, the members determine their ministry as each discerns his gifts and mission. These "callings," supported and encouraged by the entire membership, come to fruition as the ministry and program of the church.

Let the Apostle Peter give a final word of instruction to the emerging Church in this matter of spiritual gifts: "Each one, as a good manager of God's different gifts, must use for the good of others the special gift he has received from God. . . . so that in all things praise may be given to God through Jesus Christ, to whom belong the glory and the power for ever and ever! Amen" (I Peter 4:11, TEV).

4. Taking as our principle the conviction that God's presence among His people is our primary resource, let us not fail to consider that the life of the congregation in the emerging Church will probably be structured around small groups of believers. That is, the interrelationship of people in dialogue is the means by which Christ may most clearly make Himself and His purposes known. In contrast to such dialogue groups, formal classes depend on the content being taught and the ability of the teacher to communicate. The small group which takes seriously the presence of Christ can operate with or without curriculum, and with or without a well-trained leader.

For corporate worship, most churches actually depend on secondary resources — the skill, natural ability, and homiletic training of the pastor. In the emerging Church, a new kind of preacher is coming into his own for whom there is presently no adequate training. He effectively expounds the Scriptures, relates Biblical truths to the contemporary scene, and illustrates his sermons with recent experiences from within the life of the congregation. Classical illustrations from other cultures and former centuries will find only limited use in the new sermonic approach.

Moreover, recognizing that Christ indeed dwells within His people, the pastor will enable members of the congregation to participate in worship in an effective and meaningful way. Some will take actual leadership, but all will be involved in ways proper for the priesthood of all believers.

How might this be accomplished? Early in the worship service, the congregation may greet one another with some approximation of the "holy kiss" of the New Testament. There will be an opportunity to report on specific instances of God's experienced grace. These reports on God's activity in the ordinary life of His people will give substance to the prayers of thanksgiving in which many of the congregation might participate.

The real concerns and needs of the people will be shared openly so that prayers of intercession and petition will be in terms of the life needs of this particular worshiping family.

Following the sermon, in whatever form it may be presented, the worshipers will have an opportunity for dialogue with one another and with the preacher so that God's word might be related to the specific situations in which each one is then living. Members will be encouraged to report those "nudgings" of the Holy Spirit which may indicate the beginnings of a new ministry or a new challenge to be undertaken. Others who share that specific concern, or who feel a particular responsibility to the person reporting, could then meet together during the week to pray for and with him and his growing insight, until sure guidance is received and steps of obedience are taken.

6. As a traditional church chooses its leadership, more often than not the selection is made on the basis of demonstrated skills and abilities. Older, long-faithful members are usually chosen for whatever board is to oversee the "spiritual life" of the congregation. "Business types" are elected to boards that have to do with finance and property.

These skills and talents may be important as secondary resources, but they are not primary. Much too often we have seen trustee boards lose their way because business skill is all that is brought as resources to such a board. Christ does not choose only the elderly, the skilled, and the shrewd as His dwelling place! The young, the excited, the often-wrong, the untried are also people in whom He dwells. Board members in the emerging Church will be chosen first as Christ's men and women so that the primary resource of the resurrected, indwelling Christ may be brought to bear in the area of church government.

Gordon Kelly has painted a striking mural for the Yokefellow House in Defiance, Ohio. It depicts Jesus surrounded by the twelve. In the midst of this group, Philip has turned his eyes away from Jesus and is looking up into the heavens as if waiting for some spiritual experience from a God who lives "out there." The artist's meaning is quite clear: at the very time God had become incarnate in human flesh, there were those who missed what He was up to in the here and now because they were waiting for some mystical experience from outside.

This is something like our own day. Christ is here among His people in an amazing way. Instead of being aware of Christ *here*, we look for Him among the learned, the well-trained, the ordained, the charismatic. But once we take seriously the words of Paul, ". . . the secret is this: Christ is in you . . ." (Colossians 1:27, TEV), we begin to discern Him at work in the most extraordinary ways in the most ordinary people.

Christ alive in our time and in His people is a primary resource for the emerging Church. Now, what about the second of the two primary resources we see for the emerging Church: *humanity?* To introduce this concept, let one of us tell a personal experience:

> More than once I've been stumped, without an adequate answer to another person's need. But Julian really bothered me because he seemed to hurt so much. One day in the midst of a

casual conversation, I turned to him and asked, without knowing why, "Julian, how are things *really* going with you?"

The immediacy and vehemence of his response caught me off balance. "It's been real hell — for six long years." With little prompting, he began to tell me about what had happened six years before. It seemed like such an innocent thing: a friendly drink with a fellow worker. Julian was not a drinking man; he didn't even like the stuff; but the two of them had just completed a successful business venture and a celebration was certainly in order.

Driving home, Julian had an accident. His car was hit from behind by another car that was going well above the speed limit. Actually, Julian was not at fault, but the smell of liquor was on his breath and that was all that was necessary to convict him of "driving under the influence." A brief news report on the front page announced Julian's personal failure. This was certain to be well read and remembered, because everyone in town knew Julian. He was a leader in his church, a Sunday school teacher, a faithful choir member, and to top it all, a member of one of the town's "first families."

His embarrassment knew no bounds. He was embarrassed not only for himself but also for his family, his church, and all those who had counted on him. And he could not forgive himself for what he had done. When I saw him, Julian had been living with his guilt feelings for six years. He was no longer in the Sunday school or the church choir. In fact, he was not in any position of leadership in his church or in the community where he was so desperately needed.

As I listened to his story, it made me ache to realize how much time he had wasted and how much needless pain he had endured. But how do you communicate grace and loving forgiveness to a man like Julian? His friends and co-workers had tried to communicate forgiveness, but apparently in terms that didn't come through.

Julian knew the Biblical record as well as I did. He had a good grasp of theology. Intellectually he was aware of God's forgiveness for other men, but he could not apply this comprehension to his own situation. He could quote Jesus' words and Paul's teachings, but they did not seem to have Julian's name on them. When a man knows the message of the gospel and desperately needs to apply it to his own life and yet cannot do so, what is there left to say?

As I waited for Julian to exhaust his self-denunciation, I thought of my own failures and of the times when I, too, found it difficult to accept God's free grace. Then I shared with him something of my own failures over the years, and specifically one incident which was far more serious than the occasion of his arrest for drunken driving.

I spoke as a fellow sinner, but one who had personally accepted and experienced God's forgiving love through Jesus Christ. And somehow, communication took place. If an ordained and moderately successful pastor could fail badly and be forgiven, perhaps Julian could experience forgiveness also. Right there and then he prayed, "Lord, thanks for forgiving me, too. I'm sorry that I've taken so long. Now let's make up for lost time! Amen."

He was a free man once again.

What resource was available for a needed ministry to Julian in this situation? The secondary resources of theology and Biblical knowledge had not been effective. The primary resource of God Himself dwelling in the people of Julian's church was not even sufficient in this case. The second primary resource, our own humanity, was needed. God's good news needed to become incarnate in a person who had experienced forgiveness before it could be communicated to Julian.

Far too often, however, we have felt uncomfortable and guilty when our humanness expressed itself.

The experience of a young pastor in Texas illustrates this perfectly. He and his wife were in the midst of a rather warm discussion about some inconsequential matter when the doorbell rang. The visitors were a young couple, church members, who had stopped by unexpectedly for a brief visit.

Immediately the pastor and his wife stopped arguing and became the very picture of a loving couple: smiling, warmly accepting of each other, free in conversational exchange. The visiting couple never knew that an argument had been taking place just seconds before. Soon they left, and the pastor and his wife picked up the argument right where they had left off.

What a difference it would have made if they had allowed their humanity to show! Imagine the response if they had been able to say, on answering the door, "Bob and Jane, we're glad you came. We're having a quarrel and we need someone to hear us out. Will you help us?"

But because they could not let their humanity show, no help was brought to their own situation. Moreover, the visitors took nothing away from that exchange but superficial pleasantries. Perhaps they had aches and pains of their own which might have been brought out and alleviated if the pastor and his wife had been honest and open. The four of them might well have discovered a deeper relationship — separately in their marriages and together as co-workers in the Kingdom.

How commonplace it is to depersonalize the Christian message, style of life, and expressions of worship until all that remains is a kind of "sacred sterility." For example, our services of worship tend to be functionally perfect: each prayer, hymn, and Scripture reading in its accustomed place, never deviating from the printed schedule in the hands of the worshipers. The ushers or deacons follow a prescribed pattern for seating the congregation and receiving the offering. So trained are we to "the orderliness of worship" that intense embarrassment results from forgetting a hymn or putting something out of its proper place. Human warmth is reserved for the "greeters" who (also on schedule) officially welcome worshipers at the door of the sanctuary before the service begins. In many churches, this official greeting seems to be a substitute for any real fellowship within the sanctuary walls during the hour of worship.

But if orderliness and precision are essential to the church, moral perfection is even more so, according to the unwritten code for clergy and lay leadership. Moral failure on the part of church leaders, when it becomes known, results in public disgrace and usually demands the resignation of the sinner from his leadership post.

This unspoken demand for perfection, coupled with the universal fact of human failure, has had a twofold effect on the Church. First, each church member and leader is forced to live in quiet desperation with his own private imperfections of thought and deed, ravaged by feelings of guilt that can neither be acknowledged nor healed through the loving ministrations of the Christian community. Second, this thin veneer of perfectionism is seen by outsiders — especially the young — for exactly what it is: a cover-up of the real moral, ethical, and attitudinal failures which are the common lot of man *and for which the Gospel came into being in the first place!*

In our masquerade of goodness, we have drained much of the meaning from the atonement of Jesus Christ, for if we are so good, we don't need that kind of forgiveness. One result is that the more honestly sinning world outside the church door turns away from the church and looks in other directions for a word of forgiveness. The world knows that forgiveness is in short supply inside the church walls.

The late theologian Paul Tillich had something pertinent to say on this very subject:

> And now let us look once more at those whom we have described as the righteous ones. They are really righteous but since little is forgiven them, they love little. And this is their unrighteousness. . . . The righteousness of the righteous ones is hard and self-assured. They, too, want forgiveness, but they believe that they do not need much of it. And so their righteous actions are warmed by very little love. . . .
>
> Why do children turn from their righteous parents and husbands from their righteous wives, and vice versa? Why do Christians turn away from their righteous pastors? Why do people turn away from righteous neighborhoods? Why do many turn away from righteous Christianity and from the Jesus it paints and the God it proclaims? Why do they turn to those who are not considered to be the righteous ones?

Often, certainly, it is because they want to escape judgment. But more often it is because they seek a love which is rooted in forgiveness, and this the righteous cannot give.*

Strangely enough, we seem to be just as intolerant of personal success as we are of human failure. When a job well done elicits a complimentary remark, we can seldom respond without embarrassment. Instead of simply saying "Thank you," we find it necessary to parry the compliment with arrogant self-deprecation: "It wasn't me, really; it was the Lord's doing." How refreshing it would be to hear one of God's stumbling saints say, "Thank you. I was pleased with the way I handled that, too." Our humanity is usually the means by which God gets His work done. Would that we honored it as much as He does.

In the emerging Church, we will "give God the freedom" to use the humanness of His people. Demonstrated forgiveness and reconciliation will be commonplace because sin and failure, as well as success, will be more readily shared in the fellowship of the family of God. Indeed, we can say that openness and honesty to one another will be the norm of the Christian community in the emerging Church.

This more transparent relationship will take seriously the fact that no one alone can fully understand himself. Fellowship is essential to adequate self-awareness. This can be expressed in a simple diagram, adapted from one published by M. J. Sander-

|  | What I know about myself. | What I don't know about myself. |
|---|---|---|
| What you know about me. | Revealed Self | Blind Self |
| What you don't know about me. | Hidden Self | Unknown Self |

* From Paul Tillich's sermon, "To Whom Much Is Given," published in *The New Being* (New York: Charles Scribner's Sons), pp. 13-14.

son in his book, *The Journey of Being* (copyright 1966 by M. J. Sanderson, 1260 Clark Way, San Jose, California 95125).

That part of me that both you and I know is simply what I have openly revealed to you. Indeed, most of this area cannot be hidden, for it is what is apparent to the most casual observer. It is the obvious me that "hangs out" all over the place, and it is usually the limit of my relationships with others.

The part of me of which I am aware but which is unknown to you is my hidden self. Into this area go most of my failures and negatives. I don't like this part of myself, and I hide it from you for fear that you will reject me or judge me as harshly as I do myself. What is hidden in this area tends to disable me, just as a headache can make the whole body seem out of kilter. I urgently need you to share this part of me so that my failures can be seen in their proper perspective, reduced to their right proportions so that perhaps I am able to deal with them. Moreover, revealing this part of me keeps me from projecting my own failures and lacks onto others in judgment, anger, and resentment.

Moses provides us with an early example of a pattern we have learned to follow all too well. When confronted with God's challenge to "tell old Pharaoh to let my people go," Moses began to list all his liabilities: "I'm not as close to God as I should be. . . . I don't have any real evidence of a personal experience with God that others will recognize. . . . I don't have enough talent or ability to do the job" (Exodus 3 and 4). In the same tradition, whenever we are challenged by a new opportunity for meaningful involvement with others or to a deeper dimension of ministry, we immediately think of all the reasons why we ought not rise to the occasion. We list everything wrong with us and in us, spelling out our negatives in capital letters.

Unless we are in a faithful company of God's people who recognize our inadequacies but affirm our strengths, we will continue in this pattern, doing only those things which we have already succeeded in doing well. More and more we will limit our activities to what we are comfortable in doing, and the new thing into which God would send us (fling us!) is closed to us because of our obsession with our inabilities.

The third part of my being contains what I am blind to but of which you are aware. Primarily, this has to do with my strengths and abilities. Sadly enough, we are usually more sensitive to what is wrong in us than to what is right. Unfortunately and unwisely, we find it difficult to think good thoughts about ourselves.

The authors of this book have proved this time and again in conferences by using this simple demonstration with those in attendance:

> Take a piece of notebook paper and jot down five words which symbolize for you five different qualities or characteristics which you do not like about yourself and which you wish were different. Time yourself to see how long it takes to do this.
>
> Then, on another piece of paper, write down five words which symbolize five qualities or characteristics which are your strengths. Time yourself in writing these five words. Which took longer?

Regardless of what kinds of people attempt this exercise, we have discovered that the majority will list their negatives within forty seconds. Almost no one takes more than a minute. On the other hand, the same group will still be trying to list their positives after a minute and a half, with two minutes not unusual.

When discussion follows this brief test, invariably there is evidence of a sense of discomfort in talking about personal strengths and capabilities. Indeed, we have often heard sentiments such as this expressed: "But I have always heard that it is wrong to think well of yourself."

How distorted our thinking has become! To think positively about ourselves, to accept our strengths as they really are, is to give high praise to the One who created us and authorized these qualities. To affirm the high quality of a product is to offer exquisite praise to the Manufacturer!

Because I have been so brainwashed as to feel guilty when considering my positive characteristics, I urgently need you to help me see them and to affirm these strengths as mine (even though God-given). Unless you help me to do this, my continual denial of strengths will relegate them to disuse. As my brother in Christ, you owe me an introduction to — and an affirmation of — my hidden self.

Turn once again to the diagram on Page 66. Notice that it indicates an area of my life of which neither you nor I are aware. This area may be unknown, but it is not unknowable. It is the "foreign mission field" within the self. If we choose to live apart from the experience of a meaningful and affirming fellowship, the unknown will probably remain so. But if we are in open relationship with one another with the kind of mutual trust that allows me to reveal to you my hidden self and allows you to introduce me to my blind self, bit by bit the unknown will be uncovered to both of us. In this process, each of us becomes more of the whole person that God wants him to be.

This unknown self is the source of the frequently-asked question: "Who am I, really?" The common error is to assume that the unknown self may be uncovered without coming to grips with the hidden self and the blind self in the encounter of Christian fellowship.

The emerging Church will encourage and enable this kind of relationship, aware that the humanness of the people of God is one of the Church's primary resources. But now the question needs to be asked: "How might we expect this human resource to be expressed?"

*1. In the clergy-laity relationship.* The clergyman in the emerging Church will recognize that he is part of the laity (*laos* meaning the people of God) and the layman will acknowledge that he is a minister (that is, "servant") along with the clergyman. The too-prevalent notion that clergy are "different in kind" will give way to the concept that clergy are different only in function.

In Wes Seeliger's whimsical but brilliant treatise on "Western Theology," the clergyman is seen as the cook of a wagon-train in the Old West.

> He never confuses his job with that of the trail boss (God), scout (Jesus Christ), or buffalo hunter (the Holy Spirit). He sees himself as just another pioneer who has learned to cook. The cook's job is to help the pioneers (churchmen) pioneer.*

This analogy suggests that we need to do away with the double standard which demands absolute purity of thought, word, deed, attitude, feeling, intent, motive, and desire for the clergy, but permits something more earthy for laymen. This is not to say that moral and ethical standards for pastors are to be compromised. Rather, it refuses to establish a hierarchy of ethical-moral standards on the basis of ordination. If a thing is wrong, it is wrong for all Christians, both clergy and laity. If it is right, it is right for all.

There will be no second-class citizens in the emerging Church. Neither will there be "professional Christians" through whom the rest of us live out our faith vicariously. Our pastors must be as free to fail as are the rest of us. And, in our struggles together, in weakness and in strength, the *laos* will live as the forgiven sinners that God's saints are intended to be.

*2. In the honest admission of failure.* As a corollary to the above, the emerging Church will rediscover the healing power of confession. Personal failure is not acceptable to the Church today partly because we cannot tolerate our own failings. The damnation we impose on ourselves is projected as severe judgment on others of the church family who fail.

In the early days of the Church, confession was conducted openly in the presence of the whole congregation. At its best, the congregation's acceptance and demonstrated forgiveness of the sinner incarnated God's acceptance and forgiveness. The

---

* Wes Seeliger, "Western Theology" (pamphlet; privately printed). Reprinted in *Faith at Work* magazine, March, 1970.

people of God could assume their priestly role and proclaim with assurance and boldness, "In the name of Jesus Christ, you are forgiven." Those who know experientially the love of God in the midst of failure are those through whom God can communicate His forgiveness most effectively.

Compare this kind of open confession with the innocuous and impotent "general confession" intoned by most congregations. Such abstract generalizations bring no assurance of pardon because there has been no real awareness of confession.

In the emerging Church, the honesty of real confession will be provided for in layman-to-layman encounters of various kinds, in small caring-and-sharing groups of all sorts, in clusters of people within the sanctuary during worship services, and in an extended listening ministry which will involve laymen and clergy as they participate in "the priesthood of all believers."

*3. In the ministry of touch.* Jesus set an example for us which we have largely neglected. His touch was sacramental as His hands reached out to the broken, the ill, the despised, the sinful, as well as to friends and children. He felt compassion for those around Him. He said, "God loves you." And the touch of His hand confirmed that both what He felt and what He said were true.

All of us use touch in a hundred ways to convey love and compassion. We extend a hand in welcome; take up a crying child in our arms; hold the hand of a sick friend; embrace a grief-stricken neighbor who needs a shoulder to cry on; take each other's hands in a circle of prayer; give a hand of assurance to the child with whom we walk down a darkened street.

And in the emerging Church, we will acknowledge our brothers and sisters with an updated form of Paul's "kiss of peace," concerning which he often exhorts the readers of his letters. For some of us, this is already an accepted custom, particularly in situations other than worship services. Why not also as a part of our worship?

Such a custom was demonstrated meaningfully among a congregation gathered in the Daylesford Priory in Paoli, Pennsylvania. At the close of the sermon, just before communion, those leading the service moved out to mingle with the worshipers. With each person seated along the aisle, an exchange of peace was given. The forearm of each worshiper was grasped lightly and he was addressed by name: "John, the peace of Christ be with you." The worshiper then responded, "And with your spirit, Joseph." Then each person seated on the aisle turned to the person next to him and repeated the greeting, and so it continued until all in that row were greeted with the peace of Christ.

In the meantime, the worship leaders moved up and down the aisles, repeating this gesture. The gentle hum of voices greeting one another in this way gave evidence of a real sense of community that provided a proper setting for the sacrament of communion which followed.

*4. In the ministry of witness.* Worship services at St. Stephen's Church in Houston, Texas, contain a unique feature. One or more laymen are asked to report briefly on what God has been doing in and through them recently. In no way is this a retread of an earlier generation's "testimony meetings," which were too often weathered stories of someone's long-ago conversion. The congregation at St. Stephen's Church hears brief reports of current happenings: front-page news of what God is up to among His people. "Witnesses" speak extemporaneously of God's involvement with them in job situations, in family relationships, in community and social involvement, and in situations of failure and brokenness.

As a consequence, what is said is "grist to the mill" for the other worshipers. They can identify with the witnesses and perhaps find hope and direction for their own needs.

But if laymen give "news reports," the pastor can add "editorials." A witness would not preach, nor would he wander into the area of principles. He would report events as they have occurred in his own experience. The pastor may then use his sermon to editorialize in terms of principles, and exhort the congregation toward a particular goal. Nevertheless, the illustrations are those taken from the life of people either within the family of believers, or those very much like them.

Through lay witnesses, the prime resource of our humanity is most effectively used in citing real-life situations, frustrations, failures, accomplishments, and experiences of God-given freedom. This is part of Jesus' promise to us: "I came that they may have life . . ." (John 10:10, RSV).

In too many instances, the Church has neglected its primary resources: the *divinity* of Christ continuing His incarnation in His people, and the very *humanity* of those in whom He continues to live. Occasionally, a part of the Church, or a church-related activity, will rediscover the importance of one of these major resources. But the emerging Church will be radical in its emphasis and dependence on both — the resource of Christ's continuing divinity and the resource of our persistent humanity. With these as its major resources, "the gates of hell shall not prevail against it."

# PART III

## DEVELOPING STRATEGY

# 5

# OUTMODED
# STRATEGIES

The morning mail brought a newsletter from an experimental church congregation in Texas. In an article entitled simply "Change!" the editor writes about the church's goals and strategies — without mentioning either word:

A church should not change just to be different. It should change because the context of culture about it requires its organizations to restructure themselves so church tasks can be effectively fulfilled.

We believe the purpose of the church is to bring men to Christ, teach them to discern their new identity as disciples, and equip them to bring men to Christ. Worship, training, study — all must contribute to the redemptive task!

West Memorial Baptist Church is set in an area destined to be a sea of apartment houses and better-than-average homes. Traditional forms of evangelism will not effectively reach these unchurched, although they would probably attract the *Baptists* of the area. If we intend to realistically proclaim the truth of Christ's redemption to *nonevangelicals*, we must have a significantly different form of outreach. This, in turn, requires significantly new forms of training and study. Organizational structures not deliberately geared to prepare us and effectively carry out our witness would be revised to a more functional format.

Our experiment assumes total involvement of its members. It emphasizes *koinonia*, rather than purely "social" activity. It believes the church should be squarely in the world of human need, not inside Holy Walls. It shrinks from buildings, and sees the lifeblood of the church as flowing through *people*, not the arteries of educational building walls.

Moreover, it is committed to be a guinea-pig for denominational agencies who desire research projects in church life to be tested. . . .*

This particular congregation meets for worship in an elementary school building, which also provides classrooms for its church school program. Wednesday evening worship services and other midweek activities are held in homes. The only property owned by the church is a small farm some distance away, donated by one of the church families as a place to develop a training retreat program for church members.

Of primary interest and importance to us, however, is the fact that this congregation has defined its tentative goals (which may be revised or refined later) and begun to develop a strategy to accomplish those goals. It remains to be seen whether this experimental church will be able to withstand the tendency of all churches to concretize a once-valid strategy into an inflexible program "for all ages."

Basically, church strategy seems to fall into two general categories: first, those often-frenzied attempts to meet urgent specific needs; and second, the perpetuation of yesterday's strategies that might once have been valid but which now have become "programs-demanding-support" rather than "means-that-enable."

Like all organizations, churches sometimes find it necessary to develop on-the-spot strategies to meet current needs that arise without warning. The urgency of the situation itself, or a new opportunity for service that comes to light in the community,

---

* From the newsletter, "Touch News" (undated), published by West Memorial Baptist Church, 14827 Broadgreen, Houston, Texas 77024; Ralph W. Neighbour, Jr., Pastor.

may demand immediate response. Or a new project is espoused by a strong and vocal lay leader. Or a new pastor comes on the scene with some particular interest for which he seeks the support of the congregation.

It is from such ordinary stuff that church strategy often grows, and just as often, haphazardly! Such emphases need not be wrong, of course. Indeed, God may use them to work His will into the life-stream of a church. However, we must recognize that the kinds of strategy developed to handle unanticipated needs are often poorly planned, short-lived, and dependent on the attention span of the most vociferous supporter. If a church responds only to scattered and disconnected stimuli, and does not develop long- and short-term strategies based on a knowledge of its resources and well-thought-out goals, its ministry will always be inadequate.

Look at the budget of a church with which we are familiar and you will see the problem begin to come into focus. Here is a long list of mission causes and individual missionaries scheduled for nominal gifts from the benevolence side of the church budget. Each of these missionary enterprises is included because some member of the congregation has taken a personal interest in this missionary or that mission field over the years. Out of deference to these personal interests, the governing board of the church has provided token support in many different areas. As a result, the benevolence budget is fragmented and a large number of worthy causes are receiving inadequate financial support. If the total amount were applied more strategically, a few critical missionary activities would be tremendously strengthened by this one church's contributions.

Another church comes to mind: a congregation that has an endless number of committees, spawned by the governing board to meet particular needs which have arisen over a long period of time. No overall strategy coordinates the concerns and interests of the congregation. It is as if everyone were going off in a different direction at once. Meanwhile, the over-arching purposes for which the church was created suffer for lack of proper attention and planning.

Equally inadequate for the Church of the '70's are those strategies which have been inherited from the past and perpetuated without questioning whether they are valid for our time. Some of the inherited strategies which need reevaluating today are:

*Preaching.* This has been touched on elsewhere in this book; here we shall add only that this function needs to be restudied in the light of these kinds of questions: What is to be preached? What form should preaching take to make communication maximal? Where should the preacher be physically in relation to the congregation? What means of response should be provided for congregational participation? What measurements could be used to determine the effectiveness of a preaching ministry?

Suffice it to say that doing a thing because it has always been done is not an adequate reason for continuing it in the church. The function of preaching — its form, responses, and measurements — needs to be evaluated afresh.

*Church or Sunday School.* So sacrosanct has the church school become in the congregational program that to raise questions about its validity seems just short of heresy. Unthinking church members assume that there has always been a Sunday school since New Testament days. This is simply not so! Less than two centuries ago, Robert Raikes developed a strategy to meet the urgent needs of the "ragged ruffians" who inhabited Britain's slums. He found an effective way to bring the good news of Jesus Christ to those who otherwise might never have heard it. From that small beginning, the church school has grown until now it demands a large proportion of the church's physical facilities, vast numbers of trained leaders, and enormous expenditures by the major denominations for the development of curricula. And all this is done without asking the basic question: "Is this the best strategy for the teaching ministry of the Church?"

At least a few congregations have experimented with new forms of church school "classes." One that we know of has developed two experimental groups. Each group consists of three complete family units, one family unit which has only one parent, and one older adult of grandparent age. These experimental groups meet during the week in the homes of the participants. The adults share leadership in teaching when the entire "family" gathers. After a period of study, the younger children are free to play on their own while the adults continue the discussion on their level.

In this arrangement, children who have only one parent are able to have an experience involving whole families. Grandparent figures involve themselves with foster grandchildren. More importantly, the family unit in a home context becomes the basic unit of Christian education.

Recently a California pastor wrote, enclosing with his letter an eight-page summary of discussions in which he has been involved on "Goals for Adults in Church Education." This summary begins with an outline of "Some Facts and Assumptions Regarding Life in the '70's." There follows an excellent statement of "Goals in the Coaching of Adults within the Church" (having specifically to do with a style of life rather than program participation). The third section of the summary is headed, "What Program Strategies Will Actualize These Goals?" It makes a good case for thinking through an adequate strategy:

> The sort of life style I have described as our goal cannot happen simply because good organizational planning is done. Of necessity these goals require a strategy more akin to leaven than to lumber. We therefore are talking about an approach which is relational more than organizational, which is caught from one life and shared with another. . . .
> Our basic strategy is to involve persons in a small group of fellow strugglers. There may be only one group or as many as 25 or 30. . . . The life of the small group, its activities, will incorporate: fun and sharing, prayer and study of the Bible and other

books, outreach and personal growth, mutual support and task-
oriented action within the community. . . .
    We will offer additional short unit (3-8 week) studies. . . .
Persons not electing the small task-group orientation still need
sharing, study and growth opportunities.

The summary's closing section provides "Leads for Local
Church Leadership" and insists that the pastor(s) and a significant number of the official board members be involved in such
adult groups. "Pastors may need help in experiencing this style
of life themselves, not merely conceptualizing it. . . ."
    This is the kind of radical rethinking of strategy required for
the educational ministry of the Church of the '70's.
    *Worship Services.* Again we raise this subject because noth-
ing in the church schedule is so freighted with the burdens of
yesterday as the "eleven o'clock morning worship hour." Most
of our churches have a locked-in strategy for worship, whether
it is bound by missals and books of common prayer as in liturgi-
cal churches, or by unthinking habit and custom as in the "free
churches." In either case it is difficult to rethink strategy to
provide services of worship and praise that are truly meaningful
for contemporary man.
    For our purposes here, let us concentrate on three of the
many factors involved in a worship service: *the company of
worshipers itself, the language of worship,* and *the music of
worship.*
    Whatever the style of architecture represented by the sanc-
tuary in which you worship, there is historical precedent, theological justification, and ample emotional support. The Gothic
cathedral, with its sweeping lines and vaulted arches, lifts the
eye and mind of creaturely man to the heights of God's glory.
And the cathedral's modern counterpart perpetuates the divided
chancel, centering the altar-communion table as the focus of
worship in remembrance of the sacrifice of Christ.
    A less liturgical 'tradition will insist on a central pulpit to

emphasize the primacy of the written and spoken word of God, while those of an "immersionist persuasion" will focus on the baptistry in response to the Great Commission of Matthew 28:19. Be it ornate and heavy with symbolism or plain as a frontier meeting-house, the logic of architectural choice is usually grounded in a traditional understanding of worship.

If we insist on going back to something in the past, perhaps we should go back to the beginning, rather than getting off conveniently at some 18th-century plateau (or 16th or even 12th). Let's go all the way back and rediscover a hillside in Judea, a sandy shore by the Lake of Galilee, a lecture hall in Ephesus, a cellar-like compartment in the catacombs of Rome, and one of a thousand one-room hovels scattered all over the Mediterranean world of New Testament times. Whatever the physical setting, there was no "theology of architecture," but an essential fellowship which worshiped its beloved Lord *together*.

No rigid pews separated the brethren from one another; no false dignity forbade warm greetings among the faithful; no mimeographed liturgies suppressed what was normal and spontaneous; no stop watch determined the precise moment when worship began and ended.

Rather, there was celebration of a living Christ and His quite astounding victory over personal failure and death. There was an assurance of belonging — to God and to one another. There was an openness of home and purse to the specific needs of those within the fellowship. There was a building of heart-and head-wounds, and an encouragement to go back into the world as leaven and salt and light, to transform, flavor, and illuminate the way for others.

The word to describe this worshiping fellowship is *together*. Theirs was *common* worship; they partook of *communion;* they lived in *community*. Luke could write, "The group of believers was one in mind and heart. No one said that any of his belongings was his own, but they all shared with one another everything they had" (Acts 4:32, TEV). The context of worship was not a *building* but a *community*. The building was inconsequential; the community was essential.

It takes little discernment to conclude that we have reversed this order in the Church of today. The building is very important to us. If we don't have one, we feel almost homeless and rootless until we mortgage ourselves into one. If we do have one, we soon will need one that is larger and "more worshipful" — the adjective itself giving us away. (A building may be beautiful, well-planned, tastefully decorated, but only a *congregation* can be worshipful.)

The language used in worship services today also reflects more concern for antiquity than for contemporaneity. Prayers are offered, not by people expressing worship in conversational words and phrases that even the young could share, but in a stylized language reserved for the sanctuary; suggesting, of course, that worship is totally worship only within this context.

How at variance with the New Testament this is! There, the language originally was *koine,* the Greek spoken in the street and in the marketplace (as distinct from the classical Greek of the philosopher and historian). Scholars tell us that Jesus apparently spoke in Aramaic, the common language, and prayed with people in that tongue rather than in the Hebrew used in the Temple in Jerusalem.

The special prayer-language we use is a hand-me-down from the days of Shakespeare and King James and Queen Elizabeth I, via the Authorized Version of the Bible and the Anglican Prayer Book. At that time it was customary to use the words "thee" and "thou" to address a neighbor or friend. "You" and "your" were reserved for royalty. The King James Version, therefore, refers to God in pronouns normally used familiarly for a friend or companion — not in terms customary in court.

Over the years, perhaps reflecting democratic influences, the pronouns of royalty became the pronouns of everyman so that we now use "you" and "your" in daily conversation. But the printed English Bible, authorized in the 17th century, reflected no such change. "Thee" and "thou" were retained as pronouns referring to the Almighty alone; an influence reflected even in the extemporaneous prayers of today.

In a second grade church school class, it was discovered that the words "thee" and "thou" were utterly without meaning to the youngsters. On hearing this, the pastor of the church determined that never again would he use these "foreign words" in public prayer. He wanted to use terms that even the youngest worshiper in the congregation could find meaningful.

The following Sunday, therefore, he began his "pastoral prayer" using conversational language. Old habits soon intruded, however, and "thees" and "thous" found their way into the company of "you" and "your" in unholy disarray. The pastor found that he could not pray in ordinary English but kept falling back on a special language replete with Shakespearean terms such as "shouldst," "wouldst," "believeth," and "thine."

The frightening implication to this pastor was that seminary training was a requirement to learning the church's language of prayer — a perfectly obvious explanation of why prayer is so difficult for non-trained laymen. It took a deliberate process of retraining before he could converse with his God as friend to Friend. But what a difference this new freedom in prayer made once the language barrier was broken!

The music of worship provides our third example of the need to rethink the strategy of worship.

Not long ago one of us attended a large gathering of Methodist laymen. It was full of vitality and authentic representatives of the growing lay apostolate in our day. But one jarring note was that all of the hymns sung (with great gusto!) were from a bygone era; many, of course, written by Charles Wesley.

Interestingly, the fresh and authentic ministry of the Wesleys in their day was due in part to their contemporary hymns and working strategy. What they did and wrote in their time was unacceptable to the bulk of the established Church simply because it was new!

One of man's sins, even among believing Christians, is the tendency to be reactionary, glorifying the past and always looking over his shoulder. (Let us learn from Lot's wife!) The Wesleys, in their radical obedience to Jesus Christ, let the contemporary Christ express Himself through them in new words and forms. But what have so many generations of the followers of the Wesleys done? They have sanctified the words, ways, methods, and tunes of the Wesleys. Tragic!

If Charles Wesley were to return today, he would doubtless scrap his old songs and write new ones. John Wesley would probably not hold "camp meetings." Rather, he would find new ways to evangelize, recruit, teach, and train Christians, ways based on the cultural and sociological and technological pressures and opportunities of the present. To be 20th-century Christians in the tradition of the Wesleys, we ought not copy their words and deeds, but emulate their spirit and style and sense of adventure. In their day they heard the great, unchanging God say again, as He said to His faithful people almost three thousand years ago, "Behold, I am doing a new thing. The old is passed away; do you not perceive it?"

The emerging Church may follow General Booth of the Salvation Army more closely than Charles Wesley in the matter of hymnology, putting new words to singable popular tunes. Because the melody would be familiar, a congregation could sing songs that came out of life experiences of the past week, substituting a mimeographed sheet for the traditional hymnbook.

At a recent conference we had just such an experience. One of the conference participants had written verses to the tune of "Do Re Mi" from *The Sound of Music*. It was a fresh and exciting expression of praise to Christ, growing out of the experience of that very weekend, and we sang it together as part of the Sunday morning worship service. This kind of thing could become a common and meaningful experience in the emerging Church if we are able to free ourselves from the habits and restrictions of a bygone day.

All of which is to say that a strategy which is devised only under the pressure of immediate needs and opportunities, or which is no more than an echo of a strategy that once was valid, is inadequate for the Church of the '70's. There must be a better way of carrying on the ministry of Christ's Church — and there is!

# Chapter 6 ||| EFFECTIVE STRATEGY

A few days ago we went on a weekend retreat with a number of Christians from all over Ohio. Among those in attendance were fifteen men and women who were all members of one church, mostly married couples with a few single people. To use a current idiom, these fifteen were really turned-on Presbyterians, and they became a catalyst for what God did in that weekend retreat.

The fifteen were a very "mixed bag," each one different from all the others. There were liberals and there were conservatives, theologically. Some of the couples were well-to-do, others were people of very modest means. Though we did not go into political affiliation, it is safe to say that there were both Republicans and Democrats in the group. In terms of personality, they ran the gamut of types and interests. Despite all these differences, the fifteen had several things in common.

Each of them, in their church, had heard an exciting message from the pulpit. They did not pretend that their minister was a plaster saint or a paragon of virtue; in fact, one of the men said that their pastor succeeded in only about ten percent of the things he set out to do. Nevertheless, in that congregation the pulpit was alive and offering a challenge.

At the same time, each of the fifteen was meeting in small groups with other members of the church for weekly Bible study, prayer, the sharing of experiences, and mutual encouragement as they attempted to do new things for God in their daily lives.

Remarkably, the church from which they came is a small church located in an extremely small town. The church building has been described as "quaint." Yet here was the emerging Church, coming in force to a retreat to share life and the newness of life, bringing exuberance, joy, tears, laughter, and a deep sense of commitment to Christ and to His world. Here were church people who were discovering the strategy of God in their communal life; the evidence to the rest of us was overwhelming. Even more amazing was the report that in this church of about two hundred and fifty members, nearly half of the members were involved in this kind of program, centering in small groups and the discovery of the lay apostolate.

It seemed that God was telling us that there are no impossible places or churches or situations. The emerging Church will make itself evident wherever there are faithful people and clergy to respond to the new thing that Christ is doing in our time.

In thinking about strategy, it is interesting to note that in former days differences beween denominations (and between individual churches within a denomination) could be seen in the divergent emphases on theology, or on the presence or absence of certain emphases on ethical values. Today the thing that differentiates between churches is not theology or even values so much as strategy.

It is in a church's discernment of God's strategy at any given time that it may become an exciting, warm place where life bubbles up and spills out, while other congregations continue to do the same old thing in the same old way with very little happening. One might say that the basic difference is in whether a church is trying to produce settlers or pioneers — to use Wes Seeliger's terminology.

In the early decades of this century, one of the great hindrances to God's new thing happening was that denominations followed the practice of developing a strategy "at the top" and passing it down to congregations like a set of blueprints. Happily, this practice seems to be at an end. More and more denominations are discovering that, at best, denominational leaders can offer guides and resource material, but not strategy. The programs that must emerge as strategy are discovered locally, at the grassroots.

For the writers of this book, one of the most remarkable features of the gospel of Jesus Christ is its emphasis upon the uniqueness of every individual. This as much as anything else gives hope in relevant terms to people today. We are surrounded by movements that seem to make people conform to established patterns. Even those who are in rebellion against society seem to look, sound, act, and perhaps smell like one another.

Only in the gospel do we find a force and a power which encourages and enables people to become uniquely themselves. Greek scholars tell us that the Biblical injunction to "be perfect" actually means, in the original language, that you are to become the "perfect you" that God has made, unlike any of His other creatures.

We believe that a congregation, in that it is an organism rather than an organization, has a uniqueness and a personality and a soul all its own. The emerging Church realizes that every local parish, in order to be faithful to its Lord, may become unlike every other parish. Its components are unique: the forces that surround it are dissimilar to all others, its opportunities are highly individual, and "the face of its enemy" takes on distinct features. To be faithful to its Lord, a church — like an individual — must be itself.

For some years we have had the privilege of visiting literally hundreds of churches all across the land. In thinking about these various churches, it is clear to us that each one has a unique personality and a unique emphasis in mission.

One affluent parish, situated in the midst of a rapidly deteriorating neighborhood, decides to stay put rather than flee to the suburbs. Its emphasis becomes one of bridge-building between people of different races and cultures, between affluence and poverty.

Another church chooses to remain small, never seeking to enlarge its membership but keeping a unique fire burning that gives light and warmth to thousands of other churches throughout the nation.

A third congregation discovers a serious lack in its area in terms of the spiritual healing ministry. Without abandoning other programs and projects of merit, it becomes a resource to all other churches in the region through an emphasis on spiritual, mental, and physical wholeness.

Still another parish becomes deeply concerned about social issues. While continuing to administer the sacraments and provide spiritual help for individuals, it becomes known for its compassionate concern for certain displaced and disadvantaged groups in the community.

And so the list goes on. The point is that a church, like an individual, must have a distinct personality and a highly specialized emphasis that makes it different from all other churches at that moment in history.

But to say that every church must be uniquely itself is to tell only part of the story. We conceive of an over-arching strategy that will bind together all local congregations which are a part of the emerging Church of the '70's. From our point of view, this strategy — this grand design — is the emergence of the lay apostolate as God's primary means of accomplishing His will in the world. This will be the primary concern of every vital church regardless of its shape or size. All aspects of its life — services of worship, training, teaching, fellowship — will contribute to the enabling of the emerging lay apostolate.

The First Presbyterian Church in Bethlehem, Pennsylvania, has asked itself four questions:

1. What kind of laymen are we trying to deploy in the world?
2. What kind of church deploys that kind of laymen?
3. What kind of official board makes possible that kind of church?
4. What kind of clergy makes possible that kind of official board?

These are good questions for any group of concerned Christians to tackle. But note that to find a program, you begin with the end product and work back from there. The end product is always a trained, converted, equipped, knowledgeable, loving lay apostolate that Christ is producing through the many services offered in a local congregation.

To be authentic and effective, such a lay apostolate must be made up of men and women who are equipped to be three things: to be evangelists, to be healers (or reconcilers), and to be prophets. Every layman must be equipped to be *all three things.*

For one to be an evangelist simply means that he is ready and able, whenever the situation is right, to introduce another individual to the living Lord. To be a reconciler or healer means that he continues his Lord's ministry by serving as a bridge between warring, disagreeing, or non-hearing factions. To be a prophet (in the Biblical sense) means that he discerns where society is crushing an individual or group, declares that this is displeasing to God, and acts to change oppressive laws, systems, circumstances, or conditions.

When churches begin to produce laymen who can be evangelists, healers, and prophets, an authentic New Testament strain emerges which is as timely and relevant as tomorrow morning's newspaper.

Assuming that the end product of every unique congregation in the emerging Church is this three-dimensional lay apostolate, let us explore together a strategy by which God might bring it into being.

Life together for a vital parish in the emerging Church will have at least four ingredients: *worship, small groups, a retreat program,* and *training.*

*1. Worship.* Every community of believers needs a time of worship together when every expression of praise, adoration, thankfulness, dependence, and interdependence can be used to undergird the lay apostles for their everyday ministries.

At the Ohio retreat mentioned earlier in this chapter, new hymns were written by participants for the Sunday morning worship service, expressing what had been happening during the retreat. The tunes were familiar, but the words were marvelous and new, not only ministering to those of us who were present but encouraging us to be the people through whom a creative God could speak and act afresh.

Worship should not be a sterile repetition of old forms that were once vital, but a new and continuing experience of the encounter between God and man and man and his fellows, through preaching and the sacraments, through music, fellowship, prayer, and all the ingredients of meaningful worship.

*2. Small Groups.* A second ingredient of life together must be the encouragement and enabling of small group fellowship meetings.

It is true that small groups do not automatically bring vitality, nor do they necessarily encourage people to become lay apostles. A group can be sick, deadly, oppressive, sterile, or unreal. Nevertheless, we do not know of a single church now producing live laymen that does not have at its heart some form of small group fellowship.

In small groups, whatever they are called or however they are constituted, there must be several components. At some point in the weekly or bi-weekly meeting there must be a time when people can open their hearts to one another and talk about their past failures and present hopes. It is through this ministry of confession one to another (which is affirmed again and again in Scripture) that we find God bringing healing to His people.

The priesthood of all believers does not mean that we do away with priests, but rather that we become priests one to another, and by our prayers and attitudes pronounce absolution in the name of Christ.

There must also be a place in the small group for dialogue and encounter wherein members can discern gifts among one another which might never be discerned otherwise. It is amazing how limited we are in seeing ourselves without the help of others. Each of us who begins to live with a few others as unto Christ begins to find out things about himself that he would never see alone, in private worship or meditation.

Moreover, in groups people can give gifts to one another in the name of Christ. This principle, foreign to most modern-day Christians, is illustrated vividly in the following incident:

> It began as a game. A group of us who knew each other well pretended that we possessed a magic wand which enabled us to bestow whatever gifts we liked on one another.
>
> Beginning in a lighthearted way, we mentioned gifts of material things, personal characteristics, spiritual qualities — all based on needs we could readily discern. But soon the game became more serious. Out of a growing insight into one another's needs and a desire to be of real help, we bestowed "gifts" designed to fill subtler, more basic, deeper needs.
>
> At the end, each of us accepted and claimed one of the gifts he had been given, telling why it was his choice. Then we prayed, expressing our thanks to God, and a strange quiet spoke our appreciation for one another. In a sense, what we had pretended to give had actually been given — as if a Power had been at work among us of which we were scarcely aware.
>
> A troubled friend was given the gift of holy boldness, which he claimed in grateful prayer. Since then he has confirmed that something far more transforming than mere psychological manipulation has taken place in his life.
>
> A young housewife in the same group, who was losing her zest for life because of constant criticism from an ill-tempered husband, was given the gift of vulnerable love, which she quietly

claimed in prayer. Now, months later, word has come of a great
change, not only in her, wherein she could absorb her husband's
barbs without reacting, but also in him. Her new willingness to
be vulnerable has begotten a new marriage.

At first glance, it might appear that we were simply affirming
one another at points of need or deep desire, drawing on our
comradeship to apply the power of suggestion to a remarkable
degree. Or were we doing business with God Himself? Was
something profound taking place without our realizing it?

The Church knows a good deal about talents. Indeed, there
is a tendency to seek out talents among church members and exploit them. But we need to learn a great deal more about the
spiritual gifts with which God has equipped His people. You can
help someone else to discover God's gift to him. Sensitive awareness, patient listening, the fellowship of prayer, and being available — these are what Christ wants of us. With such a response
on our part, the spiritual gifts can be recognized, developed, and
put to use in great and powerful ways.

A third ingredient of small groups must be that the members
are encouraged to find the particular thing to which God is calling them for the week ahead. God's voice can be heard in Bible
study and prayer and the sharing of experiences and insights.
As in the old Wesleyan class meetings, members can be encouraged to discover God's will for them in the days ahead and to
affirm it in prayer with the others in their group.

The power of God is wonderfully administered to individuals
in the small group, so that they are both healed and enabled to
become the people who can tackle the problems of life, for themselves and for their fellows. Keith Miller calls this "the power of
the personal." It is in the power of the personal that we find the
power of God most concretely transmitted.

One form of the small group that has been particularly meaningful and helpful to us personally can appropriately be called a
"covenant community." In such a group, the members commit
themselves to one another in certain specific, mutually agreed
upon ways, for a given period of time, after which the terms of

the covenant can be reviewed or the covenant dissolved.

Both of us are presently part of a covenant fellowship which meets usually once a month for an entire day. (For some in the covenant, this requires many hours of travel.) When we get together, each of us knows that at least three questions will be asked of him:

*How goes it between you and your spouse?*

*How have your relationships been with your children?*

*What accounting of your ministry have you to make?*

Other concerns will be shared and other questions may be asked, but these three are certain to be asked in one form or another.

As often as we have been tempted to give up this covenant because of the pressure of time, we continue in it because we sense that we urgently need what such a community alone can offer:

*Accountability.* In this fellowship of concerned persons we must be accountable for what we do with our time, our resources, our families, and our ministries. No one is trustworthy enough in these areas to go it alone.

*Encouragement.* A relationship with such interested comrades provides encouragement when the going gets rough and affirmation when we get overly critical of ourselves. There are times when we simply need others to share our hurts and struggles in a helpful and healing way so that we can go back to the battle with a renewed zest.

*Help in decision-making.* A trusted group of companions can pray with and for us when costly decisions have to be made. We can think of nothing more frustrating than to be totally alone when faced with a crucial choice or decision. Again, none of us can be trusted alone to make proper choices or to discern rightfully God's will in certain instances. We trust our covenant community to discern these directions more accurately than any of us could in isolation.

*Prayerful undergirding.* Faithful intercessors will hold us before God's throne of grace day by day for healing, refreshing, equipping, enabling, and strengthening. If we are not consistently being held in the prayers of others, we will be of limited usefulness to the King and His Kingdom. The intercessions of others are channels of unlimited power on our behalf.

*The sacrament of laughter.* This is a community with whom we may discover the sacrament of laughter and play. Once each year, our covenant fellowship takes a day or an evening, or both, for dinner together and the simple enjoyment of one another — much talk, little of anything "religious," and a good deal of holy hilarity! We have not forgotten the priorities for clergy which were necessary for the "renewal" of the Coventry Cathedral parish: first, prayer; second, play; third, work.* How we have confused these priorities in the Church today!

One word needs to be added at this point. We are certain of the value of the covenant community concept especially because the clergy are involved. It is not enough for a pastor to encourage others to participate in small groups or covenant communities. As a fellow-discoverer, he must himself become involved because he needs it as much as do his parishioners.

*3. Retreat Program.* The third major component of a church's strategy should be a regular retreat program. A retreat (a misnomer enshrined by usage; it could better be called an advance) is a time set apart — one day or several days — for members of the church to dream together about the future, for their personal lives, their families, their community, their congregation, and the world. Big business calls this brainstorming; the Bible speaks of dreaming dreams and seeing visions. This is a vital method of raising hopes and of seeing issues clearly.

A retreat is also an occasion for members of a congregation, meeting in small groups, to encourage one another to be free to fail. In the warmth of a caring fellowship, one can find the courage to move out and attempt things that may not work. If a

---

* Stephen Verney, *Fire in Coventry* (Old Tappan, N. J.: Fleming H. Revell Co., Inc., 1964).

church is not trying things that sometimes fail, it is not living by faith. But if we are to attempt the things that may fail, we must have a place to stand (in Elton Trueblood's phrase); a place to which we can return for encouragement and comfort and then for the nudge to launch out again.

In dialogue in a retreat, Christians can ask one another the questions that probe the very secrets of personality and the mysteries of life and uncover some of the spots that are almost always concealed. We know of one such group where the leader asked, "What would you do if you knew that you could not fail?" This question so disturbed one couple who were present that the husband eventually left his job and with his wife took up a unique ministry in leadership training. Such questions stir up gifts and uncover blocks, thus leading to various kinds of healing and new adventures in ministry.

The legitimate use of power is something that can be discussed and discovered in a retreat. Certainly much of the power that we have comes directly and obviously from God, but each of us has the power of simply being a free person in society — free to use his power responsibly for Christ. In a retreat we can find how to multiply our power by acting together; moreover, we can discern through dialogue with others how the use of power can become blackmail.

*4. Training.* The fourth component of a church's strategy should be the use of regular training classes. By classes we do not mean the formal groupings of a conventional church-school. We are thinking in terms of a lay academy or some other regular training session that demands study, homework, and meaningful projects.

A church we know of recently named a "task force" to evaluate its adult education activities and to recommend new directions for the '70's. One recommendation under consideration is a cooperative three-year experimental program involving all the churches in the community. During this period, each church would declare a moratorium on adult programming except for the development and equipping of local church leadership (church officer training, teacher training, small group leadership training, and new member study groups).

This recommendation provides for the establishment of a community Christian Lay Academy to coordinate, plan, and implement adult Christian education for all the churches. It would require a full-time Dean of the Academy, a creative curriculum planning and governing board representing the various participating churches, and an adequately-paid teaching staff. The suggestion has been made that such an Academy meet in a non-church setting in order to make a complete break with the past so that the three-year experiment could stand on its own merit. The cost of the Academy would be underwritten in part by the participating churches and in part by tuition fees charged to those attending.

If a layman is to become free to serve in a maximum way, he should become acquainted with theology and history, and he must be aware of current trends that spell out opportunities for the day.

Churches must be more serious about the kind of teaching and training they offer. There is a need in the emerging Church for clergymen who are tougher, harder, and wiser than the clergy we have known in the past. We must have men who can train and equip the laity for the hard task before them.

The decade ahead is wide open for churches that see themselves as centers for recruiting, training, and equipping a breed of spiritual pioneers competent to move out into all areas of life as lay apostles who can evangelize, reconcile, and prophesy. This, in our view, is truly the apostolic succession.

# PART IV

# DISCERNING OPPORTUNITIES

# Chapter 7

# OPEN DOORS

On the day we began to write this chapter, the *New York Times* carried a story about a seventy-four-year-old Japanese who had left his wife and son in 1937 and who was recently discovered in a mountain cave where he had lived for twenty years. He rejected pleas from his family to return home, stating, "I am much more comfortable living in the cave."

This could be a parable of much of the Church in our time. Frightened by the prospect of becoming involved in the changing tides and pressures of everyday life, the Church has too often hollowed out its own cave where it could remain untouched by the world, setting up its own rules of conduct, ethic, and style of life. To become enmeshed in the problems and stresses of culture, politics, economics, and changing morality has seemed a sure way for the Church to lose its purity and possibly its very identity.

In the town where we live, a church has recently been constructed whose architecture is striking: it is built in the shape of an ark. The builders of that church are to be commended for their honesty in representing architecturally what the Church has all too often been in actuality.

Communities of believers, anxious to remain faithful to their

Lord, have built strong theological and ecclesiastical walls around themselves to keep out the winds of change and controversy. This "ark theology" is perhaps the greatest enemy the Church has to face in our time. We are grateful to see that it is changing and that a whole new stance is evolving.

It is our conviction that God is a God of order and logic; that He has a plan for His people which can be fulfilled if they discover their proper goals and make good use of the resources available to them. But this plan also takes into account the cultural, social, and political opportunities of any given time.

One key to the pattern of the emerging Church in this decade must certainly be found in its eagerness to discover and respond to the amazing opportunities that surround it. Swift, dramatic changes and developments in contemporary society pose no threat to the Church in its life and ministry. Actually, each change provides a thrilling new opportunity. Let us take a brief look at some of the obvious trends in America today and see how each can be viewed as a rich opportunity for the Church.

*1. The decline of Christianity.* It is quite obvious today that Christianity and the Christian Church are less popular than at any other moment in this century. This can be seen in declining church attendance, declining budgets, and in the scorn and disinterest in the Church demonstrated by so many young people today. This attitude is summed up in four words emblazoned on a picket which a young man carried to a Billy Graham rally in California: "Christianity No! Jesus Yes!"

How different this attitude is from the one which prevailed among concerned young people when the authors of this book were in high school and college. Then the Church had popularity, but Jesus was a name no one mentioned in polite society. The change in attitude is, we think, a very healthy one. Now the Church has the opportunity to become an open fellowship of people, living out a style of life, bearing witness to the Lord of life, rather than a closed institution in which are enshrined various attitudes, concepts, customs, and codes of behavior.

Not long ago, while conducting a preaching mission in a local church, one of us was given hospitality in the home of a couple who were members of the congregation. They had a son who was a "hard-core hippie." He had dropped out of college during his senior year and gone to work for underground newspapers, first in the Boston area and then in the Haight-Ashbury section of San Francisco. He took LSD and had adopted the ethics, convictions, and general style of the people with whom he lived and worked.

In the evening this young man would stop by for conversations with the visiting preacher. He was not the least bit interested in the Church as he saw it and had been raised in it; but he was interested in Jesus Christ. He wanted to know what "hard-core Christians" really believed to be Jesus' goals, purposes, and general life style. The Church was irrelevant to these conversations, but not the Lord of the Church!

Vast numbers of individuals, both young and old, are quite indifferent to the Church because of what they see as its conventionality, lack of interest in real human problems, adherence to the status quo, and reluctance to confront institutionalized evil in society. Yet many of these people consider themselves religious, or at least open to truth wherever they may find it. What a fantastic opportunity for the emerging Church if it can recover the simplicity of the gospel and the strategy of Jesus Himself!

*2. The youth revolution.* Today's young men and women have values which they are eager to affirm, righteous anger which they are willing to express, and power which they are able to use. By seizing the moral initiative in our society, they have set in motion one of the most exciting and hopeful developments in memory. Yet to many, the youth explosion signals the end of civilization as we know it and the inevitable destruction of all the values we have traditionally affirmed. What is the real truth? There is no simple answer, yet the emerging Church can regard this development as a tremendous opportunity.

Of course there is a lunatic fringe among youthful activists. The most "radical" seem as doctrinaire and reactionary as Stalin himself. Those who cry "Fascist!" the loudest are hardly distinguishable from the Hitler Youth of the thirties. But let us not be misled into believing that the extremes of right or left are representative of the vast majority of young people who are shaking up our world.

Despite their noise and self-styled radicalism, youth today are deeply conservative in the best sense of the word: committed to the preservation of human life and natural resources. They reject the drift and hypocrisy of their elders, for they will not accept different sets of standards for various groups within the nation. At heart they are passionate reformers, far more sane and humane than many of their elders, even though they have a tendency to seize on slogans and simplistic answers.

The emerging Church can hardly ignore these young people. It will either see them as a threat and shut them out (which would be suicidal) or it will listen to and learn from them, meanwhile holding high the banner of the true revolutionary, Jesus Christ.

*3. The new morality.* This is a catch-all term, but to most people over thirty it signifies just one thing: an erosion of traditional sexual morality. Whether our sexual habits have *in fact* changed greatly in the past thirty years is impossible to know for certain, but unquestionably there are more people today than ever before who declare openly that they do not accept either the Victorian ethic or the hypocrisy which accompanied it. In 1970 it is quite possible to imagine this kind of conversation taking place between a frantic father and his college-age son:

*Father:* You kids and your so-called new morality! It's nothing but an excuse to sleep around and do as you please.

*Son:* Dad, you don't hear a word I say. I never said I approve of promiscuity. I said I didn't see anything wrong with premarital sex under some circumstances.

*Father:* Well, what's going to happen to family life if there aren't any promises or legal boundaries?

*Son:* Your generation hasn't done so good with preserving family life. Half your friends have been divorced and remarried.

*Father:* We're not talking about other people, but about us. To think that a son of mine is on the road to hell . . .

*Son:* I don't believe in hell.

*Father:* But the Bible says . . .

*Son:* What part of the Bible are you talking about?

*Father:* St. Paul clearly says that fornication . . .

*Son:* Everybody knows that St. Paul had an aversion to women. Anyhow, if you're going to quote the Bible, how about all those sexual rules and regulations in Exodus and Leviticus? You never mention those, but they're in the Bible, too. Do you think we should stone adulterers to death?

*Father:* But that's the Old Testament . . .

*Son:* Just like you, Dad. You quote the parts you approve of. Well, nobody I know is going to have his life regulated by some stupid rules that may have made sense two thousand years ago.

*Father:* But you've got to have rules. Where's your sense of responsibility?

*Son:* I *do* have rules. The right thing is the loving thing; that's it in a nutshell.

*Father:* That won't help you much if your girl gets pregnant.

*Son:* Are you kidding, Dad? Everybody knows how to avoid pregnancy.

*Father:* And supposing you get a venereal disease?

*Son:* Supposing I do? A few shots of antibiotics will clear that up soon enough.

And so the father and son go round and round, never hearing each other and never coming close to the real issues involved in sexual morality. The son has a point in that to hold to a morality out of fear of consequences — in the present or hereafter — is no morality at all. The father has a point in that there must be commitment and responsibility in love if it is to endure and be satisfying.

The emerging Church must learn to speak to both sides of the generation gap as regards sexual morality. It must affirm that the real reason for sexual purity has to do with the dignity of man and with our respect for one another as individuals. The new moral climate gives us a chance to affirm old truths and to call people to true freedom and responsibility within the family of Christ.

*4. Emergence of an informed laity.* Another great opportunity for our time, which seems a threat to "the establishment" in the organized Church, is the rise of an informed laity. Some decades back, before universal public education and before the development of the mass communications media, people in general were less well informed than they are today. As we mentioned in another part of this book, the clergyman was a disseminator of all kinds of knowledge, not just "spiritual" insights. This has all changed today. It would be hard to conceive of a church that did not have among its faithful laity people who were better informed on almost every issue — except, perhaps, theology — than the clergyman. And in many churches there are more keen theologians among the laity than among the clergy!

This threatens the clergyman who sees himself as the great source of wisdom and information. But if we see as our goal in the Church the producing of a lay apostolate in the world, then it becomes clear that much of our task in training the laity has already been accomplished by schools, newspapers, radio and television. In this context a clergyman becomes not a disseminator but an interpreter of news. All too often the laity are inundated by news and facts and do not know what to do with this body of knowledge. The clergyman should be able to bring a Biblical light to bear on it. But more than that, he should become the coach of a team, realizing that many of the team members will have more information and be potentially better players of the game than he is. But a good coach can make all the difference, for morale, for discipline, and for understanding and interpreting facts and insights.

*5. Mobility.* Another frequently heard complaint of our time has to do with the extreme mobility of people. Especially in the suburbs one hears clergymen and official church boards bemoan the fact that they can't build a continuing program because one-third of their congregation moves every year.

This is an interesting complaint, because at the same time there are rural and inner-city pockets of people whose churches complain that theirs is a static membership where nobody ever moves. It's the same old people doing the same old thing, and it's hard to bring any kind of message or program involving change.

Obviously, the old saw about the grass being greener on the other side of the fence applies here. But we believe that to seize the initiative which is the Holy Spirit's is to realize that whatever situation a church may find itself in, there is a particular emphasis of the gospel that can be captured there. For example, a church with a highly transient, mobile membership is in a very advantageous position to work toward the goal of evangelizing the world and leavening society. This kind of church has a built-in "governor" to prevent its becoming self-centered and self-perpetuating.

Just as our Lord had no more than three years to train His apostles, so the typical suburban church of today has a very short time to call out, equip, and train its laity before they move on. If the goal of a church is to produce a laity that can reproduce itself in other people and in programs that will change and liberate society, then a church with high mobility has a unique opportunity.

On the other hand, where there are static pockets within our society, the Church has an opportunity to work in depth and to see long-term goals in developing continuing relationships and ministries. The danger in this case is that the Church may become a self-perpetuating club or ingrown little family. But the opportunities far outnumber and outweigh the dangers if we can capture the depth of the gospel in terms of becoming a model for a new society.

6. *Affluence*. Neither of the authors of this book has had the privilege in recent years of occupying the same pulpit Sunday after Sunday. But we have had the compensating privilege of visiting a great number of churches across the land. All too often from pulpits we hear decried the danger of affluence. It almost seems as though affluence is the greatest enemy that true spirituality could have! Of course, there is good reason to believe this, as one recalls the proverbial eye of the needle and the camel struggling to get through. But on the other hand there are many stories of affluent people in the New Testament, notably those whose funds enabled the first communal experiment in the Church. We must remember, too, that one of the two men who claimed our Lord's body from the cross was a man of means.

However, it is not usually the few people of extreme wealth who are seen as a threat. Rather, it is the general affluence that elevates the middle class. The great bulk of Americans are becoming more and more affluent, while the hard core of the really poor become more and more imprisoned in their poverty.

The danger is that the increasingly comfortable middle class, who make up very largely the membership of churches, will rely more and more on material security and neglect their Christian responsibilities. Any gift can become our undoing. We all know the cliché of the struggling newlyweds for whom poverty and uncertainty were the marks of true faith and true romance. When affluence and success came, faith went out the window, romance dwindled, and the marriage broke up. This familiar story sums up perfectly what happens to many churches as well as many marriages.

The other side of the coin cannot be ignored, however. Affluence creates leisure and leisure provides a great opportunity for the Church in terms of the lay ministry. Long before their retirement, people today have more time at their disposal than ever before, and they wish to make use of it. Leisure becomes a threat if people merely use it to improve their golf or bridge scores, or begin to drink more and enjoy it less.

But think of the increasing numbers of concerned and committed Christians who are using their leisure for ministries through small groups, community involvement, and personal evangelism. Leisure can be a great gift if the Church is able to harness the will and motivation of its people for Jesus Christ.

7. *Mingling of the "sacred" and the "secular."* Another characteristic of our time is that the wall which has separated the secular from the sacred is crumbling. A great many sermons have been preached on this subject during the past decade. It is as if the Church were afraid that when the walls come tumbling down, you won't be able to tell the ark from the world. The implication is that the world will penetrate the Church and rob it of its purity and uniqueness. Perhaps this threat is real, but it seems to us that the typical reaction is not only very defensive, but also one which runs counter to the whole thrust of the Kingdom of God that Jesus has established.

If the Church is truly on the offensive and aggressive in its war of agape (selfless love), then when the wall comes down which has separated the secular from the sacred, the Church militant — with its equipped, informed, converted, trained lay apostolate — will be able to penetrate the world with its message of the risen Lord and His plan for individuals and for the world. When the wall comes down, the Church is free to move out with its message into the very bloodstream of society.

This is the very opposite of the ark theology, with its determination to conserve or preserve something from the world's destruction.

Actually, the Church is meant to be a society against which the gates of hell cannot stand. In this figure of speech we see the Church not holed up behind gates, resisting the battering of the world, but moving out from its stronghold of worship and attacking the very gates of hell that imprison people spiritually, socially, economically, or psychologically. The Church must be in the world as salt or as light, leavening, illuminating, infiltrating, attacking.

More profoundly, we must realize that in this situation, when the wall no longer exists between the secular and the sacred, it is the world for which Jesus Christ lived and died and for which He now longs. When the veil of the temple was rent, it was not only an indication that Jesus' death on the cross opened a new access to God and made available the holiest of holies to man. The reverse was also true: that God was no longer confined to the sanctuary, but was loose in the world to do His relentless and ruthless work of challenging, confronting, forgiving, redeeming, releasing, and enabling men to be sons of God.

Far from being a threat, the disintegration of the wall between sacred and secular is a fantastic opportunity for the emerging Church.

*8. Depersonalization.* Another strong current in our society is that which tends to depersonalize individuals. Oftentimes men and women today have lost their very names. They are reduced to numbers — on checks, social security cards, draft cards, charge accounts, utility bills, and addresses. The population explosion seems to mean that individuals count for less, and only movements have validity. This recalls the old Marxist cry that people exist only for their society.

As Christians we believe just the reverse: that society and government exist for individuals. There is some truth in the simplification that the scientific approach seeks to help people by improving the mass, while the Christian approach tends to improve the mass by helping individuals.

Again, the situation presents the Church with a unique opportunity. In a society where the climate is impersonal, how much more relevant is the eternal gospel of Jesus Christ, who lived, died, and rose again for individuals — one by one, in tens, or in millions. Individuals have worth, and Jesus Christ has come to redeem men that they might be "more unique" than they could ever be without Him.

There are no stereotypes in the Kingdom of God. Rather, the Kingdom is a fellowship of unique individuals becoming even more unique (a psychological if not a grammatical possibility) as the centuries roll on. Thus we see that the Church can claim a relevance in our society because of the winds that blow depersonalization. When it comes to calling men and women to discover their unique personhood, the Church has never been more needed than it is today. Proclaiming this dimension of the gospel should give it a hearing all across the land. And this will bear rich fruit if congregations show evidence of a corporate style of life that bears witness to the worth of individuals.

So far in this chapter we have briefly discussed trends in society which may be seen as threats to the Church but which actually represent opportunities. The list could be greatly expanded. Our purpose is to call attention to a primary task of the emerging Church: to discover its opportunities and take advantage of them. But how can it do this?

For one thing, we can tune in on the knowledge explosion which not only makes available a colossal amount of information about the world of the present but also forecasts future trends. It would be foolish indeed to close our eyes and our minds to what is happening in our world and what is likely to happen. Recognizing this, one church leader more than a year ago presented a prophetic paper on the world of the '70's, based largely on a report prepared by one of the largest business concerns in the United States. This corporation had asked a selected group of its top officials to forecast trends of the '70's so that the corporation might manufacture and merchandise more effectively. In preparing this report, the corporation interviewed economists, political figures, sociologists, management figures and industrial relations experts.

The church leader perspicaciously seized on this forecast and shaped a forward-looking plan for his denomination, utilizing the business acumen and "secular" wisdom of some of the nation's most outstanding minds.

This provides a clue for the Church. We believe that the Church must not only see current trends as opportunities, but also try to predict future developments so that it may set goals that are in keeping with God's goals — for He lives in the future as well as in the present and the past.

When the Church in any era fails to realize that a changing trend is an opportunity and fails to seize that opportunity, then there usually springs up some movement alongside the established Church to capture that ground. In our time one example of this is the growing strength of the behavioral sciences. This is a threat to many in the Church, and viewed with alarm. But if we listen to what the behavioral scientists are saying, we can find a new frontier for the Church.

Experimenters in the forefront of the behavioral sciences, whether they emphasize T-groups, sensitivity groups, touch therapy, or any of a dozen other techniques, are all saying that they seek to minister to a segment of the populace which is not deeply sick, psychotic, or morally off balance. They are working with the "gray" people who are unfulfilled and do not know how to live life to the full. It is the intention of the behavioral scientists to reach this middle stratum of people so that life might become full for them and they might learn how to relate to others in depth and to become fulfilled in their own beings.

It occurs to us that the forgotten people in the Church are these very gray people. They fill the pews, support the programs, and pay their tithes, but they seldom get much of the Church's professional ministry or concern. They are ignored because they are not on the verge of divorce, not having nervous breakdowns, not about to become alcoholics, not addicted to drugs. Nevertheless, these are men and women who are looking for a dimension of the gospel that will bring fullness to their lives.

In the past when the Church has been truly vital it has devoted a great deal of time and effort to ministering to those who are society's outcasts. It has reached out in compassion to slaves, drunkards, prostitutes, the imprisoned, and the psychotic. And it must not fail to continue such a ministry.

But what of those who do not fall into any of these extreme classifications? What about the law-abiding people who are dying a little every day and have never learned how to live? One of the frontiers of the Church is to realize that the bulk of the lay apostolate, as it emerges, will come from fulfilled gray people who have discovered that the gospel is good news for them and for their marriages, jobs, and neighborhoods.

The world is full of opportunities for the Church. And when the Church is true to its Lord and its divine calling, it will speak with power to those in the world who might otherwise ignore it completely.

The late Albert Einstein once said a remarkable thing. "Being a lover of freedom, when the Nazi revolution came, I looked to the universities to defend it, knowing that they had always boasted of their devotion to the cause of truth; but no, the universities were immediately silenced. Then I looked to the great editors of the newspapers, whose flaming editorials in days gone by had proclaimed their love of freedom; but they, like the universities, were silenced in a few short weeks. . . .

"Only the Church stood squarely across the path of Hitler's campaign for suppressing the truth. I never had any special interest in the Church before, but now I feel a great affection and admiration for it, because the Church alone had the courage and persistence to stand for intellectual and moral freedom. I am forced to confess that what I once despised I now praise unreservedly."

Tragically, Einstein was referring to only a small part of the established Church of that day; yet it was the part which was truly the Church. More tragically, the Church has very often failed to find the courage and persistence to stand for intellectual and moral freedom.

But the point is that the Church did speak to one of the great men of our time who was avowedly not a Christian. In being faithful, it ministered in a way it could never have ministered if things had been going well. So today we see that all of the destructive tendencies loose in the land give the Church a unique opportunity for being, for speaking, and for ministering.

Chapter

# 8

# CASE
# STUDIES

A church which is able to recognize general trends and circumstances and turn them into specific opportunities is one which will be a vital part of the emerging Church. Lacking this discernment, a congregation will either remain static, never seeming to find God's power or direction, or wallow and sink into oblivion. In a very real sense, making the most of opportunities and finding Christ in them is the most exciting adventure a church can embark on.

As individuals, many people have come alive in relinquishing to God their "if onlys." These include missed opportunities, lack of education or experience, being in "dull" situations, becoming bogged down by family or financial responsibilities, or just plain garden variety sins that can easily wreck a life. Part of the good news of the gospel is that there is no circumstance, event, or failure that can come to a person or to a church that cannot become the very resource God will use to make that person or that church exciting and significant.

How can an individual or a group of people go about finding their unique opportunities and taking advantage of them? Rather than deal in generalities only, we would like to call attention to a number of true stories and incidents which spell out the principle in specific terms. None of these examples may apply directly to your particular situation, but taken as representative object lessons, together they may suggest to you ways in which you may discern your own opportunities.

Last year, one of us was in England for a series of lay renewal conferences. At a one-week conference for teen-agers, among the majority of typical British youths who cared little about faith or about the Church there was a handful of exciting young people who had found a relevant and communicable faith in Jesus Christ. These unusual youngsters were from an inner-city Anglican church in Liverpool, where they had begun to meet Jesus Christ through their new rector only a year or so previously.

Liverpool has its own dialect, comparable to Cockney in London. This dialect, Scouse, is the language of the Beatles. When the church's new rector came to Liverpool, he could not speak Scouse and he had difficulty communicating with his parishioners. Making the most of his incapacity to communicate, he asked a group of teen-agers to teach him the dialect.

They met over a pot of tea in the basement of the rectory, afternoons when school had let out, translating portions of the New Testament into Scouse. Not only did the rector learn the dialect, but the young people through him had an encounter with Jesus Christ.

The interesting thing here is to notice that every minister moves to a new church with certain cultural or social limitations. He can "fake it" and blunder through, or he can use his very ineptness or lack of background as a bridge to get close to his people. This is very much like our Lord, who was constantly asking people for help.

A certain church in New England called as its pastor a "lay dropout" who had just completed his seminary training. It was the first pastoral assignment for this businessman-turned-clergyman. After some time, he became aware of a number of "opportunities" in the church. One of them was that there was a significant number of members who had been patients in various mental hospitals — not an unusual circumstance in the average twentieth-century parish.

Realizing that this situation was probably an opportunity rather than a liability, the pastor called some of these people together for breakfast one morning. He told them why they were there, and suggested that they could probably have a significant ministry to one another as well as to other members of the church. To break the ice, he spoke freely about some of the problems he was discovering in his own life and marriage and ministry. At that first meeting, the pastor recalls, each person had a bit of advice as to how he should handle his life!

The second meeting, a week later, found the same group gathering together, but this time they began to open up to one another about their own personal needs. Within six months, the minister reports, this group produced some of the strongest, most vital lay apostles he had ever known. They ministered not only to one another, but also to members of the church who did not share their distinctive background. Here is a clear-cut example of a circumstance that might have been ignored or swept under the table, but instead provided a rich opportunity for service.

The two cases mentioned above are on rather a small scale. In contrast, here are two accounts that deal with whole congregations — which happen to be quite dissimilar. One is a small, struggling, "ethnic" church in the heart of New York City. The other is an affluent suburban church in one of the wealthy cities of the South. The first congregation was weak in membership, finances, buildings, and other material assets, but for a time discovered how to capture strength and depth and new life in Christ. The second church had to go from strength to brokenness to new life in ministry. In the first case the story is told by a layman,

a former member of the church; in the second by a former pastor
of the church.

Many years ago I had an extraordinary experience in a
church; an experience I am only now beginning to understand. It
began when I joined an inner-city parish which had fallen in evil
days. The congregation was dwindling in size, there was not
enough income to maintain the property or to maintain much of a
program. For some time there had been no permanent pastor; a
succession of students and substitute pastors had tried to fill the
gap.

Just at the time I affiliated with this church, an energetic and
gifted clergyman of middle age accepted a call to become its pastor. He saw in the situation a real challenge, and he was determined if possible to stir up some life.

Responding to his vision, a group of us — mostly young, single people — began to devote a great deal of time and effort to
the church. Some of the programs and techniques we tried soon
failed, but through it all a sense of camaraderie far beyond the
ordinary sprang up among us.

And some of our efforts did not fail. At least in a small way,
we were beginning to feed the hungry, clothe the destitute,
house the homeless, and respond to the emotional and spiritual
needs of those who wandered in looking for help.

Many of the older parishioners who showed up only for morning worship knew little of what was going on. But faith and hope
were being kindled and this was somehow communicated in real
but subtle ways. Nothing in the conventional worship pattern was
changed, yet the services seemed more vital. Even though there
was little of a structured program for them, young people began
to "hang around" the parish house, getting to know one another,
singing in the choir, organizing a bowling team.

Little by little, among the "core group" gathered around the
pastor and his wife, camaraderie developed into something deeper
and more meaningful. Because we loved each other, we learned
how to be honest about our failures and needs. Sins were con-
fessed and in some cases dealt with realistically for the first time.
We studied the Bible, prayed expectantly, played and ate and
laughed together.

We did not realize it at the time, but it was as if a fire had been lighted in a fireplace, and more and more people began to be drawn to its light and warmth.

Within a couple of years, that parish was alive again, humming with activity. No, there was nothing avant-garde about what we did there; it was a perfectly conventional parish program. Nevertheless, everything seemed to have changed. Worshipers appeared out of nowhere, and stayed on to become active members of the church. Fellowship groups were formed and some of these were spontaneous enough so that they did not stagnate but continued, month after month, to throb with life. In short, a moribund parish had had a most extraordinary rebirth. Even the church building was repaired and redecorated.

Yet, within another few years, everything changed again. We all seemed to become very busy. There was less and less time for the core group at the center to be together in any significant way. We pursued our activities and maintained our programs, but they were becoming mechanical and institutionalized.

Then, alas, some of us at the very heart of things began to be defeated morally, and instead of facing these defeats openly and honestly, we tried to gloss them over. After all, how could we admit that we were in trouble? We were the leaders, the very heartbeat of the parish!

Secrecy and dissimulation replaced candor as drink, sexual immorality and personal ambition took their toll. Within an incredibly short time, there was a falling apart of those who had been so closely tied to one another.

None of this was obvious on the surface, yet all of us knew that something terrible had happened. One day, after months of soul-searching, the pastor offered his resignation. But this was an anticlimax, for the life had already gone out of that amazing experiment.

Occasionally now I visit that church, though I am no longer a member. Things are still humming there, in a very different way. There is a highly organized program for almost everyone who wants it. There is a far greater emphasis on social responsibility, which I find admirable. Because of several sizable legacies left to the church by faithful members now departed, there is no shortage of money. There is a competent professional staff.

But for me — and for the old friends with whom I dare to talk about the old days — none of this means very much. The parish seems now to have little to offer to the spiritually hungry. The fellowship was the fire at the center, and that fire went out a long time ago.

The second, more recent example has to do with St. Paul's Methodist Church of Columbus, Georgia. It is told by Guy Hutcherson, who at the time of the events reported was pastor of the church. Presently he is minister of the First Methodist Church in Albany, Georgia.

St. Paul's is known as the "country club church" of Columbus, Georgia. The congregation represents a high level of educational achievement and economic status. In the four years I have served as minister at St. Paul's I have discovered that prosperity solves some problems, but creates others. I have been much concerned for our spiritual life.

Our people seemed restless in their affluence. When they went to the sea or to the mountains, or traveled to the East or West, they seemed to me to be trying to get away not only from the routine of life in Columbus, but from themselves. I began to pray for a spiritual breakthrough and was led to believe that a lay witness mission was the means whereby it could come about.

Other Methodist churches in Columbus had held such missions, with Tap Hanson, a local businessman, as coordinator. Our official church board called on Tap for help.

From the start, interest in the mission swept through our church like a prairie fire. One month before the weekend set for the mission — March 8-10, 1968 — Tap Hanson met with a sixty-five-member general committee and enthusiasm was already high.

I can't pinpoint any moment or event that lighted the match; I only know we were ready, and God was ready. Here we were, adults of good standing in the community, with good salaries and education, yet one thing was missing from many lives: God. And we were becoming aware of the fact. Amid our affluence we were starving spiritually.

The weekend was organized to perfection. We invited a sixty-member team of the finest of witnesses to be with us. But when you add it all up, the results were not man-made, they were God-sent.

Things began at fever pitch with a Friday evening dinner meeting. The 350 who attended taxed the capacity of our social hall. Tap Hanson introduced people like Buddy Steele, from West Point, Georgia, and Bill Henderson, from North Carolina. Bill, who owns the largest advertising firm in the Southeast, gave the most unemotional talk I have ever heard about his running from God and being found by God — and elicited a highly emotional response.

Bill Godwin, a former University of Georgia football player, was inveigled into coming when we asked his wife to help serve dinner. He said he'd eat and leave. He wasn't going to get involved with a bunch of fanatics. I knew he felt this way, so I sat next to him. Well, Bill *didn't* leave, and he and I sat there with tears in our eyes as we listened. He kept elbowing me when some remark hit home, and in the small sharing groups that convened after the general meeting, he and many others bared their souls and opened their hearts to Christ.

On Saturday, separate luncheons for men and women were held. That evening we met together again. And on Sunday morning Tap Hanson spoke and then very quietly invited men and women to give their hearts to Jesus Christ and confess it by coming to the altar. People came by the dozens, some weeping, some laughing.

But the greatest thing has been the follow-up, the spiritual growth we've had since March. Nine prayer-and-sharing groups have been formed. Some of our people have traveled to other congregations to participate in similar missions. Many of us have discovered that we can live in the stream of a secular world with the love of Christ in our hearts. Just as our visitors in March, over a cup of coffee, in elbow-to-elbow conversation, witnessed to us about Christ, stripped off their masks and were real with us, we are learning to witness to our friends and neighbors.

We discovered that we could come to Christ as we were. One kept hearing people exclaim over this as a great revelation. And we discovered the enthusiasm that can come from living this new life together. Many of our members who did not get involved in the weekend have been drawn into the small groups by the love they have seen in those who now stand side by side in a new kind of fellowship.

Jim Ward is one. Jim had practiced medicine in Columbus for sixteen years, "competing with God," as he expresses it. "When you diagnose cases right and build a successful practice, why do you need God?" had been his attitude. Yet he knew that God was there and that there was a vacant place in his life.

As Chairman of the Commission on Finance, Jim Ward came dutifully to planning sessions for the Witness Mission, but he planned to play golf March 9 and 10. "But Bill Henderson hit me between the eyes," he says. "Then Charlie Phillips, in my sharing group. I didn't miss a meeting after that. On Sunday morning I went forward. I told God, 'Here's the greatest mess you've ever seen, but take me and do with me what you want.'

"What's happened to many of us is that we feel a tremendous responsibility. I thought commiting my life to Christ was wonderful. Now I find it even more wonderful to know that you can have some little part in helping someone else find Him. In all my years as a doctor I had never witnessed. Within ten days of my commitment, two people came into the office and asked me to pray for them.

"Then a friend of mine whose wife had come through major surgery successfully called and said, 'Jim, I'm trying to find God. I want Him to know how grateful I am, and I want Him to know how bad I've been, too.'

"I said, 'Boy, I'll be praying for you.' I thought, *Why don't you go over and help him?* But I was reluctant, and hung up without making the offer. Five minutes later my friend called back to ask, 'Doc, how about coming over here to help me?'

"So I went over and we got down on our knees and prayed. That man accepted Christ right there."

It was after midnight at the parsonage when the doorbell rang. My wife looked out and said, "It's Dr. Ward. Something bad must be happening." I ran to the door, and Jim said, "You can shoot me for coming by here so late, but I've just had an experience I have to share with my preacher." And he told me what had happened.

This is the kind of thing that is happening over and over again in Columbus, Georgia.

Here is further evidence of how circumstances can lead to the discernment of fresh opportunities. The narrator of the following true story is a Baptist clergyman with an earned doctorate in theology, who was teaching in two seminaries (one Protestant and one Roman Catholic), serving on the staff of a church, and doing an experimental ministry for his denomination. He discovered the lay apostolate by being able to receive ministry from a non-intellectual, non-theological lay person who saw his need in the area of personal relationships and dared to give him assistance. William R. Nelson, who tells the story, at the time of this writing is Teaching Minister of Lake Avenue Baptist Church, Rochester, New York. In June, 1970, he will become Program Director for the American Baptist Assembly in Green Lake, Wisconsin.

When I was ordained in 1951, I assumed that a minister was expected to have all the answers, and that it was his job to run the church. My experience as a young Christian had centered around a few ministers who were my models for the authoritarian role which I was preparing to fill.

But after completing the B.D. and Th.M. degrees, I still did not have all the answers, so I continued graduate studies. In 1956-57 I served as Assistant and then as Interim Pastor of the Clinton Avenue Baptist Church in Trenton, New Jersey. For every new insight I gained from my biblical and theological studies, a new question was raised by the sociological complexities of serving an inner-city congregation in a changing community.

The same church called me to be their pastor in 1960, after I had spent a year studying at the University of Heidelberg on a Fulbright scholarship. For five years I fought to bring a sense of hope into an almost defeated congregation. Major strides were made in sensitizing the white middle class membership to the needs of the black working class neighborhood where the church building was located. Through it all I was the aggressive leader who confronted the church with its changing community, and most of the congregation followed obediently because they trusted my judgment.

My authoritarian image was made even more secure when I received the Th.D. degree in 1963. And though during my last year in Trenton I started to talk about the role of the minister as an enabling resource for the laity, I was still locked in the "center ring" with the feeling that the whole show had to pivot around me.

In the fall of 1965 I was called to join the staff of the Lake Avenue Baptist Church in Rochester, New York. This church had embarked on a five-year program in cooperation with the American Baptist Home Mission Societies and the Colgate Rochester Divinity School for the purpose of exploring the shape of renewal in a strong, urban congregation of 1400 members.

After several months of soul-searching, I felt that God wanted me to accept this position. There were two unusual requirements in the final agreement regarding my call: my family and I were to live in the inner city where the church building was located, and I was to supplement my previous training with further courses in clinical pastoral education.

Little did I realize at the time that this experiment in church renewal would have to begin with me. My authoritarian role no longer worked because I was the youngest member of the staff, working with three seasoned professionals.

A big shift in my attitude resulted from a new sense of freedom which my wife Colleen and I found with two other couples who were also searching for the meaning of renewal in their lives. The six of us spent a weekend in Washington, D.C., where we consulted with Gordon Cosby and Don McClanen of the Church of the Saviour.

Contact with Faith at Work was established when two other men and I sought help from Bruce Larson, Howard Keeley, and Lloyd Ogilvie. It seemed to us that Faith at Work was a resource for renewal that would complement our own strong activist tendencies with a deeper sense of supportive Christian community. I knew that our success in developing new forms of ecumenical ministry in our neighborhood in Rochester would be short-lived without an effective means of equipping and sustaining the laity who were involved in mission.

With considerable ambiguity, our church decided to host a weekend Faith at Work conference in December, 1967. Though some of the language of the twenty-four visiting team members was a bit strange to us, their authenticity was unmistakable and their joy contagious. The overwhelming impression of the weekend was that the laity could be real ministers.

Because I wanted to get a closer look at this vital lay ministry, I attended the Faith at Work conference in New York City the following month. And there, to my surprise, God used a "non-theological" housewife, Lorraine O'Heren of Findlay, Ohio, to short-circuit my authoritarian syndrome.

It happened that we were assigned as co-leaders of one of the talk-it-over groups that would meet four times during the weekend. After meeting Lorraine, I concluded that putting the two of us together was like trying to mix oil and water. Her hang-up was churchy people, especially ministers. She was sniping away at the Church from the outside, wondering why everyone on the inside had such a hard time understanding her.

Since my "rank and serial number" as a minister didn't help me in this situation, my only alternative was simply to be myself. From the beginning I admitted that I hoped to revitalize my personal relationship with Christ by taking a hard look at the reality of prayer.

At this point Lorraine was eminently qualified to help me. Though her life was far from a mushy success story, it was apparent that to her God's presence was a living reality.

But as far as the talk-it-over group was concerned, it seemed that the two lead ships were approaching each other on collision course. I was familiar with relating to an intellectually-oriented Bible study group in our church, but this was my first attempt to relate to a group purely on the basis of personal Christian experience.

I had agreed to initiate the opening discussion. Of the six additional people in the group, two were familiar faces from Rochester. We all told why we were there and what we hoped to gain from the conference. Most of us were not really sure, but I summed up the discussion in such a way that it sounded profound. When Lorraine and I compared notes afterwards, it was obvious that I was carefully controlling what happened in the group, and getting in the way of free expression.

The next day at lunch my wife stopped me dead in my tracks by observing that I was running away from God and from myself. "Don't you know that you're not in charge of this conference?" she said. It was clear to her that I was still playing the role of the authority figure instead of facing up to my need as a person to find the quiet center of my life in Christ.

Lorraine seemed greatly relieved when I offered to relinquish my leadership role in the group, and our second session was free and spontaneous. A Methodist minister had dropped out of the group, and a young professional girl, Silvia Zawadski, had dropped in.

Silvia, whose background was Ukrainian, had been attending the Lake Avenue Church. She found in Lorraine one who deeply understood the blocks in her previous religious experience, and who freely accepted her as she was. By the end of that session, contact between the two of them had been firmly established.

Lorraine realized that her husband Dick had been through the same kind of dilemma that Silvia was now facing, and the three of them went out for a leisurely dinner and conversation. It occurred to me that I was observing "the priesthood of all believers" in action. Dick and Lorraine were the ministers Silvia needed: they could speak from their own experience about the thing that was troubling her most — a religion synonymous with fear.

Our third group session was unforgettable. Silvia felt free to share some of the new insight she had gained about herself. And Lorraine sensed just the right moment for the two of us to lay hands on Silvia, to give her the strength to take the initial step of personally committing her life to Christ. When we had prayed for her, Silvia responded slowly and thoughtfully, expressing her confession of faith in a halting Ukrainian accent.

As the entire group sensed the presence of Christ and the power of the Holy Spirit in that "upper room," the Pentecost story of the early Church became relevant for me. I could not explain what happened, except to affirm that God was present in our midst, healing a broken relationship.

I saw that the instrument God used for this healing experience was *not a correct theological answer, but a transparent life.* Then it hit me: the only way to break out of my authoritarian role was to shift the emphasis of my ministry *from giving answers to sharing experience.*

At the fourth session, Lorraine and I were working as a team. The experience we had shared with Silvia overshadowed our individuality with the larger perspective of oneness in Christ. I no longer needed to be in charge of everything as the pastor-director in order to minimize the threat of person-to-person ministry. In fact, the conference set off a chain reaction which has enabled me to enter into the struggle for genuine Christian commitment with several other persons.

Months later I saw Lorraine and Dick again, and we got together with Silvia for a progress report. Silvia was in the process of becoming a member of the Lake Avenue Church. I was sensing a new freedom to be an enabling minister. And as for Lorraine, she had overcome her prejudice against church organization to the point where she was serving happily as president of the Women's Society of Christian Service in her own congregation.

The priesthood of all believers is more than a doctrine to me now. The lesson I learned from Lorraine, and which I continue to discover in fresh ways, is this: when I take hands off and allow Christ to be "my boss," then He can use me as an enabling resource to equip others for His ministry.

One of the main blocks to the renewal of the Church is the clergyman who does not trust God enough to allow the laity to be ministers too. A church program which is limited to the vision, insight, and approval of one man is destined to remain onesided and ineffective.

For our final example, we turn to a large, successful church on the West Coast. Perhaps this is one of the most unusual churches in the nation; certainly it is one of the fastest growing. The story is especially pertinent because we often hear both clergymen and prominent laymen lamenting what a church has lost in becoming large and affluent. In such a case, depersonalization seems almost inevitable. But listen to Harold Leestma, one of the ministers on the staff of a wealthy church, tell what has happened to it.

We like to say that the Garden Grove Community Church is the largest, smallest church in Orange County, California. God has sent us an amazing number of people. In my job as Minister of Evangelism, I have the privilege of meeting and instructing several hundred families a year as they come through our eight-week Pastor's Classes. I try to get to know personally as many as possible, and when we looked to God for an answer to the question of personal friendships and Christian involvement for so many church members, He gave us a simple solution in His own providential timing.

The first inkling of what this solution would be came in the fall of 1963 when one of our "new couples" invited my wife and me to join them at a Faith at Work conference in Riverside, California. There we met Gert Behanna, one of God's marvelous modern-day saints. Later she came to speak to our people, and captivated the entire congregation with her honest sharing of self.

Three months later two couples from our church attended a Faith at Work conference in Phoenix, Arizona. Under the inspiration and challenge of Bruce Larson, Rosalind Rinker, and Corrie ten Boom, and in the atmosphere of small groups, the four came alive in an exciting new way. They asked us for the names of church couples whom they could invite into their homes, and we pastors supplied the names of people who had expressed an interest in adult fellowship groups.

Thus our first talk-it-over group was born. The first members were two engineers, two salesmen, two real estate brokers, a teacher, a banker, a policeman, an employment counselor, a nurse, an office worker, and six housewives. Except for one engineer and his wife, all were new to this kind of experience.

Needless to say, there were "growing pains" as together they struggled with self-discovery, group interaction, and discussion format. Attempting to put their faith into action during the two week interim between meetings made for lively conversation as they shared their victories and defeats. These were some of the questions they asked one another: How did you and God get along together last week, at home, in the neighborhood, on the job? Did you put in a good word for Jesus Christ? Did you love another person at his point of need? What did you do when the "old man" inside you picked a fight with the "new man"? Who has been on the throne of your heart this week: you or Christ?

Empathy grew among the group members as they lived their lives in close fellowship. Through shared joys and sorrows, God knit a group of individuals into a family unit. Even the children of these couples were included in some of the extracurricular group outings, and the love of Christ began to bind them all together with a deepening concern for one another.

Even in times of deep sorrow and pain, with serious illness and the loss of loved ones, the group stood firm, and together weathered life's storms. God was teaching these people right in the nitty-gritty events of everyday life. The bi-weekly group meeting became a sort of laboratory in living. No longer was the third person of the Trinity a stranger to the members: they had seen Him at work and felt Him in their daily lives. Now they could be His channel to reach others.

This is when the talk-it-over explosions began. Up to that point, recruits had been enlisted by word of mouth or pastor referral. Now the group encouraged the pastors to host a Faith at Work conference on the church campus in order to introduce this new concept to more people in the congregation. Following the conference, a second small group was formed immediately, and a third soon after. One of our couples volunteered to teach a six-week class in "Sharing Your Faith with Others." As a result, many new persons expressed a desire to continue meeting together, and two more talk-it-over groups were formed.

Our novice leaders leaned heavily on the Holy Spirit, prayer, Scripture, and Faith at Work study lessons, but now they wanted some actual leadership training. In the spring of 1967, Harold and Mary Brinig came from the East to share their experience with those of our people who were involved in small groups. For many years the Brinigs had led small groups in Marble Collegiate Church in New York City.

One dynamic weekend with the Brinigs gave our people a new shot of spiritual adrenalin. New groups popped up all over the place, as individuals found the courage to step forth and invite others. The following year the Brinigs returned, this time for six weeks. Enthusiasm ran high. Mary and Harold met with the group leaders collectively and individually; visited every existing group; hosted an open house sharing session for the entire congregation; spearheaded a team of witnessing couples to a neighboring church; and taught a course in "Faith in Action."

All this led to still more talk-it-over explosions. At the same time our leaders were growing deeper in their commitment to their respective assignments.

Our layman's leadership team has grown to seventy persons in charge of thirty-two small fellowship groups. They meet in living rooms, around kitchen tables, in coffee shops, and on the church campus. Every two months I meet with these leaders for an exciting time of sharing experiences, which gives me a chance to feel the pulse rate for each group. This leadership team is under the auspices of our Evangelism Committee, who meet with me every month to plan over-all guidance of the small group movement in our church.

The fear is sometimes expressed that home groups will become ingrown and separate themselves from the life of the church as a whole. This has not happened at Garden Grove. The home groups have helped our people to relate more naturally and comfortably to the total church program. In finding themselves, individuals are more free to lose themselves in others.

As for service in the church, it has tripled. Even very shy people are stepping forward, seeking their particular assignment from God. Believing that God has a definite plan for each life, they often can't wait to get into action.

Jesus Christ is alive! With His power working in us, we come alive, too. Live people make live churches.

Here is a marvelous example of a church that did not have to become small in order to become personal and relevant. It spells out how a congregation can seize the opportunities of the moment and make them subservient to our Lord.

Specific opportunities for existing churches are constantly expanding and proliferating. New techniques and programs which take seriously the lay apostolate, lay witness, issue-centered ministries, and the understanding and appropriation of "secular" wisdom can revolutionize the Church without destroying anything of value and give it a whole new image in the world's eyes and a whole new dimension of ministry.

# PART V

# DREAMING DREAMS

# Chapter 9 ⦀

# NEW DIRECTIONS

When Charles Darwin set out on his exploratory voyage, one of his avowed goals was to find evidence to prove that the Genesis account of creation was literally, factually accurate. To his astonishment, he discovered a wealth of evidence that God's creation is far more complex, dynamic, and fluid than the writers of Genesis could have imagined. Darwin realized, in short, that to regard the Old Testament story of creation as a scientific treatise — or notes on a laboratory experiment — was absurd. It was, rather, a superb statement of faith.

Whether the theory of evolution that Darwin eventually formulated is accurate is beside the point. The point is that he was able to see the evidence which God had set forth from the beginning — and was still setting forth. There was nothing new about this evidence. It was right out in the open, as if waiting for someone with the perception and perseverance to recognize its significance. Darwin was able to set aside his preconceptions, reevaluate his goals, and at length open the world's eyes in a fresh way to the mystery and complexity of the physical creation.*

There is a good deal of irony in the fact that Darwin, who had planned in his youth to become a clergyman, suppressed his

---

* Alan Moorehead, *Darwin and the Beagle* (New York: Harper and Row, Publishers, 1969).

ideas about the process of evolution for many years, fearing that they would shake the faith of his contemporaries. In this he was not far wrong. However, lest we look askance at the unwillingness of the Victorians to reexamine their ideas and reevaluate their goals, let us admit that it is difficult for us even today to imagine that God may be far more surprising, dynamic, and creative than our preconceived notions allow Him to be.

If this is difficult for an individual, how can we expect a church to evaluate its goals, strategies, and performance? The concept of evaluation — which we are borrowing from the American Management Association — can be given different names that sound more "spiritual," but it really would not change the concept.

For example, evaluation for a church might simply be the ability to receive new guidance from God about its particular role or destiny.

During his term of office as Bishop of Rochester, Fulton Sheen attempted, as part of a reevaluation of his church's mission, to give away some diocese-owned real estate so that it would be used to benefit poor people in the area. He was thwarted in this attempt, yet perhaps such a move *was* part of God's plan for that church at that time and in that place. It is possible — though we can only conjecture, of course — that Bishop Sheen's plan might have come to fruition if he had been able to share his guidance and his vision with a strong team of men responsible for the administration of diocesan affairs, and enlist their help and support in a radical change of policy.

Similar stories could be told of many churches in many denominations. One could speculate ad infinitum on "what might have been" in the history of the Church if there had been less of a tendency to settle for the status quo and a greater willingness to respond to changing conditions and circumstances.

This can happen only when men and women who have been given authority in the Church are able, in community, to evaluate their goals and their performance, and to scrutinize their strategy with ruthless honesty. It is never easy to do this, even for an individual. There is nearly always an element of crisis in a radical shift.

The Old Testament story of Abraham provides a vivid illustration of this. When Abraham took his son Isaac up onto the mountain to offer him as a sacrifice and thus prove his faith, he was certain that he was under God's guidance.

Obviously, the best goal that Abraham had from God was not the slaying of his son. The whole history of God's covenant people — the "Church" of the Old Testament and the Church in the New Testament — would have been different had Abraham not been able to hear God say a new thing to him. But he *was* able to change his goals, and therefore to change his strategy.

Peter, too, faced a momentous crisis when he had a vision from God indicating that he must change his attitude toward the Gentiles. The parallel between "clean" and "unclean" animals and Jews and Gentiles was obvious to Peter. Yet the concept of clean and unclean was part of the very warp and woof of his experience, training, and faith.

How shocking it must have been for Peter to hear God say that a new day had come, and that the old concept must be abandoned forever. By faith he had the courage to accept this guidance, and such was the nature of the apostolic fellowship that Peter's vision won the day and set the tone for what was to follow in the spreading of the Gospel.

Another striking New Testament example of reevaluation is found in the account of the Church's early communal experiment. Shortly after the day of Pentecost, the people of God felt that it was their goal and God's purpose for them to try to live together communally in one place, sharing their substance and drawing, according to their needs, from the common pot. Few details survive to tell us about this experiment, but we know that it ended soon after it began. Apparently the early Christians were free to fail, free to assess whether their goals were adequate, free to change those goals. Without missing one step in their faithful march of obedience, they scrapped the goals that did not prove to be worthwhile, got new ones, and moved on.

Vitality in the Church depends on its ability to change. This is not a new problem in our time, but the problem of the Church of Jesus Christ in any age. Both Old and New Testaments reveal the struggles of the people of God to adopt strategies and goals for living, speaking, and governing themselves that would be relevant to their changing times and circumstances, but would not do violence to the message from God of which they were stewards. This is true also for contemporary Christians.

If there is real life in the Church it is always the gift of God. It wells up when God's people are enabled by His Holy Spirit to discover again and again, both individually and corporately, an authentic style of life which is relevant and contemporary, while rooted in the eternal good news of Jesus Christ.

This gift of life is not distributed capriciously or erratically by God, but rather offered to *all* of His people *all* of the time. A church's ability to change its goals and strategy and then become receptive to the new thing that God is trying to do to and through His people at any given moment is the determining factor in whether it fulfills its mission. The ability to change requires prophetic discernment, self-understanding, and raw courage born of faith.

If we take into account that vitality is a gift from God, it soon becomes clear that one of the greatest things a man (or a group of men called a church) can bring to God in order to receive this gift is the ability to evaluate goals, change them, or receive new ones. Malleability such as this is centered in our openness to evaluate and to hear, either for the first time or to hear anew, what God is saying about our particular obedience to Him in any specific place at any given time.

The mark of the Christian Church in its most authentic forms is not that it always be right, but that it be capable of correction, rediscovery, reevaluation, and change. A church that rigidly maintains it has at one time received God's guidance and is now

remaining faithful to that guidance — we are not here referring
to Biblical revelation — either takes itself too seriously or else
does not understand the nature of God.

What human being or institution, even when called a church,
can assume that what it has heard at any given time is *absolutely*
what God said? Even if it is an authentic and valuable word,
the nature of God as revealed in Jesus Christ and the New Testament clearly indicates that God can do once again a new thing
and give new orders to His people.

The capacity to change is one of the most precious gifts that
a church can have. It is also a tremendous witness to the fact of
God's forgiveness in the Cross of Christ and in His continuing
presence with the Church by His Spirit. It means that a church
is not justified by always being right, but by believing God and
accepting His forgiveness. Therefore, it is flexible enough to
ask God again if it has heard right or if, having heard His message in the past, it is now performing adequately in terms of
strategy and the right use of resources.

We know of a church whose membership was dwindling as
new racial groups moved into the neighborhood. Instead of becoming disgruntled, the church divided its membership into task
forces who met one night a week for several months to study
the mission of the Church and to ask what their specific mission
should be. After determining that the primary need in their community was the development of strong Christian men, the pastor,
who had majored in education, decided to focus his ministry on
the recruitment and training of teen-age boys.

Devoting himself to the development of a club program for
boys, he literally neglected many of the traditional pastoral duties
that adult members had previously considered their due. Soon
the church was filled with boys playing basketball, attending
church school, forming youth clubs, doing service projects. Two
years later, parents were coming to church. "It did so much
for my boy I decided that I belonged here," was a typical
explanation.

Now, another year later, the church has once more divided itself into task forces to think through the next strategy. As a result, two new staff members have been added — black youth workers for boys and girls. The pastor, meanwhile, is free to give himself more fully to the needs of adults, both the older members and the newcomers, and to involve himself with the politics of the city as a way of demonstrating his conviction that the gospel speaks to all the needs of men, for forgiveness and better housing, for Bible study and better government.

In contrast to this example, it would be easy to mention churches that have spread themselves so thin in an effort to change society that they no longer have the resources to minister to the spiritual needs of individuals. The point is that every congregation must have the capacity and the willingness to examine itself and determine where it is failing and what its specific mission should be.

# Chapter 10 ||| VISIONS AND POSSIBILITIES

"Without a vision the people perish." It's as simple as that. To dream the impossible dream is to live, for without dreams people die and the Church dies. This conviction is central to what we see for the emerging Church in the 1970's.

There is nothing new about dreaming big. In the Old Testament it is prophesied that there will come a time when "old men shall see visions and young men dream dreams." This prophecy is picked up in the New Testament and becomes a key to interpreting what God did when He came to live among men (in Jesus Christ and within men (at the day of Pentecost). Toward the end of his long life, the Apostle John saw a vision of "the new Jerusalem" and wrote at length about it. Many other early Christians, whose writings are not included in Scripture, also contributed to a body of apocalyptic literature describing their dreams and visions.

Whenever the emerging Church has become vital enough to make a strong impact, there have been dreamers who saw "the big picture" in a new way. Saint Augustine wrote a magnificent book about the City of God. John Wesley and his teammates had a vision of a new kind of society, where individuals would be set free from the bondage of sin and become the leaven to change their society.

143

In our own day we have a man like the famed psychiatric pioneer, Carl Gustav Jung, talking about Jesus Christ making possible a new rung on the ladder of evolution. It is impossible to separate life in the Church from the capacity and ability to dream authentic dreams and see great visions.

Earlier in this book we expressed the conviction that a church will be defeated if it is problem-centered or if it has inadequate goals. The opposite of this is to seek a vision of what God is doing in the present, and to test this vision in the crucible of reality. The Church must be able to dream of its own shape, size, destiny, and style of life. A church that is alive must also encourage individuals within its membership to dream personal dreams about God's new thing for them. Moreover, groups within the Church must dream about their ministry and corporate existence. Families within the Church, too, need to have the capacity to dream a new dream of what God is doing in and for and through them.

Listen to what one man says about his experience as a husband and father:

> For many years in my life as a Christian I had a vision of Christ making me perfect, adequate, or simply good as a father and as a husband. My quiet time was geared to asking God for this earnestly in prayer. I must confess — and my family will happily testify to this — that this produced little in terms of effective ministry on my part to the family.
>
> In time I came to see that what God wanted me to be was someone who could be used by Him as a catalyst, so that the others in the family might find their true selves and the true nature of God who loved them in Jesus Christ. To do this, I simply had to let God make me vulnerable and honest about my mistakes in the presence of my wife and children, and to affirm them whenever this could honestly be done.
>
> This vision has given me a new freedom to be the man God can make of me in helping my family to discover its own identity and ministry.

There are countless individuals within the Church who have had a dream or vision of what God wanted them to be. For example, a certain New York businessman had his life changed by Christ. It affected his marriage, his health, and his habits. But he had a growing dream that God wanted to use him to help others outside the circle of his immediate family. His dream is being fulfilled, for he is learning how to listen to, care for, and pray with people with whom he lives and works. God is fulfilling the authentic dream given to him.

Another businessman, now in his middle fifties, has been a long-time churchman, church officer, and generally upstanding citizen in his town. Through meeting with some other laymen in a small group in his church, he caught a vision of God wanting to use him to change conditions for some rather neglected citizens in the area. In order to find the time to do this, he sold a large business and developed a very small one. This provides him with an adequate income but allows him to devote time and energy to housing problems. The vision he received has not only liberated him as an individual, but spurred him to improve the lot of a number of other people in his vicinity.

Some years ago, in a southern town, there were four men who were inseparable friends. They lunched together frequently, played golf and went fishing together, and often dined together along with their wives. Because of the jobs they held, they were four of the most influential men in that town. They represented four different churches, but all were Christians.

One day they became aware of how they could be used to help undergird and enforce the new federal laws encouraging desegregation. Quietly they began to call on those in the area who were ignoring or deliberately flouting the laws. In defiance of tradition, they dared to use their secular power to liberate black people economically and politically. Because they dreamed a dream and acted upon their guidance, at least a measure of freedom has come to disadvantaged citizens in that corner of the nation.

We live in a time when small groups are being rediscovered as a primary means of enabling both clergy and laity for mission. A small group is a place where personal healing and help can come to individuals through a sharing of experience, Bible study, and prayer. But tremendous things can happen and have happened where groups have had a vision that called them to be more than a center for finding personal wholeness. The second mile for such groups is to "spin off" individuals into mission, singly or corporately.

Men who met in small groups in a church in Wisconsin, for example, had a vision that God meant to use them somehow in a nearby prison. For some years they have sought to fulfill that vision, and as a result the lives of many prisoners have been changed, both inside the institution and outside, following their release. Not only that, but the programs instituted in that one prison have had far-reaching effects on the penal system in Wisconsin and in surrounding states.

As part of its coverage of the October 15, 1969, War Moratorium, the *New York Times* carried a brief but moving story about a young mother in Duluth, Minnesota. Between the lines of that account one could read the story of an awakening vision among a small group of Roman Catholics in Duluth. The young mother, who characterized herself as a "ghetto Catholic," had until recently never held strong political views. But through exposure to the preaching of her parish priest, through reading about the peace movement, and most of all through examining her conscience as a Christian with regard to America's policy in Vietnam, she concluded that she must join in a prayer vigil that day.

Whether one agrees or disagrees with her position, it is clear that her vision and that of her group is enormous: no less a thing than to change the foreign policy of an entire nation. We do not presume to recruit members for her cause, but we do encourage God's people to dream dreams that are big in scope.

God is in the "dream business" for the Church at large and

for local congregations as much as for any individual or group.
Every local church needs to discover that it has a general and a
particular ministry entrusted to it at any given time. This will
be contingent upon the opportunities and problems that surround
it, and the wider cultural situation in which it finds itself. As a
church is faithful to the particular thing entrusted to it, it will find
that evangelism, stewardship, and all the other usual concerns
of a parish will be taken care of along the way. But if it devotes
its time and energy solely to these conventional responsibilities,
it may never see the particular vision that God has for it.

Let's take a look at a few specific situations and see how this
principle works out in real life.

A congregation in the heart of one of America's great cities
found that it had become a little enclave of white people surrounded by an almost totally black community. Rather than re-
move to the suburbs, as so many hundreds of congregations have
done under similar circumstances, this church dared to dream
that God expected it to stay and minister to the people around it.
Radical changes were made in that parish's concept of obedience,
worship, ministry, and virtually every other aspect of its life.
But in the process it became a dynamic center for life-changing,
cutting across all social and racial barriers. In a sense the church
remains an anachronism in its community, but it is true to its
vision of what God intends for it.

Many years ago an Episcopal priest in Texas had a vision
that the new center of authority in the Church was to be a witnessing fellowship of laymen. This dream was at first reluc-
tantly and at length enthusiastically "bought" by the official
board of his church. What evolved was a program of lay witness
which is flourishing and ministering to churches across the nation.

A struggling church in the middle of New York City's theatre district had a vision that God meant for it to minister to
people of the theatrical world. Over a period of time, traditional
forms of worship were discarded or modified so that the worship
and life of the parish would be meaningful to the rather "special"

people of the community. The result is a congregation which is
unorthodox in every way, but fresh and vital. Moreover, the
members are aware that when their innovations begin to "harden"
into sterile patterns, they must again be reexamined and further
changed. It is apparent that lives are being changed and ministries discovered in this unusual church.

Another New York City parish, old and illustrious, is situated in the "East Village" where thousands of "hippie" types
and struggling artists vie for space with blacks and Puerto Ricans.
Some of these newer residents have come into the church and
altered its character from top to bottom. Unorthodox ministries
are being attempted. The traditional worship service has been
scuttled. Even the seating arrangement in the sanctuary has been
changed.

Needless to say, these changes have shocked and saddened
many long-time members of the church, and some of them have
given up and moved to other parishes. At this moment the congregation is in a state of flux, but those at the heart of its life are
certain that they have a vision of God's will for them, and they
are struggling to be true to their vision. It is not easy for an
outsider to view this church and judge whether all that is happening is good, but it is perfectly obvious that the church is very
much alive — and far from a museum piece!

A large church in a small Midwestern city has as its pastor
a man who is a great preacher and evangelist. For years he was
"released" by his congregation so that he could conduct preaching missions all over the country. Then the church and its pastor
began to have a dream about the lay apostolate. The dream was
shared in such a way that as requests came in for the pastor to
speak in some other church, he responded that the best thing he
could do was not to come himself but to send a team of laymen
who would bear witness to the mighty acts of God in their own
lives.

Now this church sends out many such teams every year to
encourage and kindle life in other churches. What is more, lay-

men of that congregation have embarked on experimental ministries, including a coffee house and a halfway house in their city. In short, what was a great "preacher-centered" church has become a church with a great preacher *and* a great laity doing a new thing in our time.

Another prosperous congregation, this one in the suburbs of Philadelphia, had a vision that it must be faithful to the concept of an ecumenical style of life. This dream has gradually filtered up from the grass roots and down from the pastor until a great many members are caught up in creative ministries, shared with Roman Catholic churches in the area and with a monastery located right across the street from the church building. Occasionally the Protestants and Catholics join together for worship. They also minister together in a school for handicapped children, share in healing services, and join forces for youth work in that town. The church flourishes as it holds faithful to its vision of the ecumenical dimension of life in Christ.

A group of churches in an Ohio city had a vision that there ought to be a church available for people who were deeply concerned about issues and conditions in that town. Therefore they called a man to come and be pastor of a church that would be built around issues, not around an edifice. The church now moves from place to place, trying always to be at the center of "where the action is." It exists because of the dream of a number of Christians in a number of churches, all of whom led members to this unique congregation.

But what happens to an "established" clergyman who has a vision that seems to call him away from his regular pattern and into unknown territory? If he believes strongly that the vision is of God, and if he has faith and courage, he will step out and seek to fulfill it.

An example of this is Ben Campbell Johnson, a Methodist minister who had a vision of lay witness teams criss-crossing the country. Ben had to leave a parish to head up the first lay witness missions. But as this book is being written, a thousand such teams are being sent across the country, witnessing in local churches to the mighty acts of God and altering in significant ways the church life of our nation.

Another minister had a vision that spiritual healing was a dimension of the gospel too much neglected in our time. Through two successive pastorates in the last ten years, he has started healing services that have had a profound effect on many individuals and also on a number of churches in the two cities in which he has served.

Recently we met a man who was the pastor of a large suburban church. Following a clergy conference where dreams were encouraged, he described his situation to us. His church was flourishing and the members loved him. He lived in a beautiful parsonage, and he and his wife each had a car. But though people respected him and his circumstances were more than comfortable, he confided in us that his dream was to go to some undeveloped country — possibly in Africa — to teach little children to read and write.

What will happen to the dream of this middle-aged, successful pastor? We do not know, but we suspect that God is in it and we pray that he may be free to leave the established and respected pattern and try the thing that may well be God's next step for him.

A young preacher on the West Coast had successfully organized two congregations. Both were thriving when he sensed that he was not as close to people as he ought to be. As an evangelist, he could speak to masses, but he felt that he could not get next to individuals. Through a series of circumstances, he met a tremendously effective layman who had a stocks and bonds business. The young man left the clergy and went to work for his new friend. Recently he confided that he has been able to lead more individuals to Christ as a businessman than he ever did as a clergyman.

It is difficult for his family to accept the fact that he left the clergy. Tragically, they cannot see that he is in every sense a minister of the gospel, only now more effective than he was before. Here is a man who dared to follow his dream and not be caught in some ecclesiastical mould or maze.

Will the emerging Church destroy the established Church? Emphatically no! When some clergyman or layman, or — preferably — clergymen and laymen together, begin to ask God for an authentic dream or vision, living out that new thing will not include destroying what has been. Rather, the new emphasis will have begun; the old vision will be left to those for whom it is still valid. But it is amazing how a few people faithful to a dream can capture others as the dream begins to take shape and becomes negotiable.

In New York City we have seen a parable of this very thing. The old Pennsylvania Station was to be razed, and the new Madison Square Garden erected on the site. For many months we saw, bit by bit, bricks coming down from the top of the old station and steel work beginning to rise from new foundations within. After several years, we have seen the old building entirely replaced by the new.

But all the while this was going on, no train ever stopped running, nor was any schedule interrupted. Simultaneously the new emerged and the old diminished. This is the kind of thing that we feel certain God is doing in local churches across the nation and around the world. To dream is not to destroy, but to build. The edifice that results from dreaming quietly overshadows the old, and in time the old may pass away.

It is the Church's responsibility to continue to minister the grace of God to individuals through worship, teaching, administration of the sacraments, calling and caring. But it is the vision that gives shape and direction, dignity and force, to all that is happening within a faithful congregation. For without a vision, the people perish.

*Guidelines for Evaluation*

Let us suggest here some guidelines to use in self-evaluation. These suggestions could be used in various ways and at various times by different groups within a church. The official board might want to use them, or the professional staff in a large church, or a group of interested church members, be they teenagers or senior adults, or a businessmen's breakfast or luncheon group.

EXERCISE 1. UNDERSTANDING YOUR CHURCH

1. Describe your church in terms of:
   a. The age groups and kinds of people who attend.
   b. The quality of relationships of its members.
   c. Its influence on the community.
   d. The meaningfulness of its worship.
   e. Its theological position.
   f. The number of active members; active family units; other important statistics.
2. What is your church's attitude toward:
   a. Tithing or proportionate giving.
   b. Social action.
   c. Conversion and spiritual disciplines.
   d. The place of young people in its ministry.
   e. The ministry of laymen.
   f. Involvement in the surrounding neighborhood.
   g. Interdenominational cooperation.
3. What do you believe are your church's strong points? Why these particular strengths?
4. What do you believe are your church's weak points? What accounts for these?
5. What have been your church's long-term goals? (Answer from what you know of its present emphases.)
6. What do you think are your church's short-term goals?
7. What is your church now doing to fulfill these long-term and short-term goals?
8. What is your church now doing that hinders these long-term and short-term goals?
9. What new goals is your church considering?
   a. Long-range.
   b. Short-term.
10. What could one individual now begin to do to help in accomplishing these goals?

## EXERCISE 2. RELATIONSHIPS

We have been talking in this book about the concern of the Church being wholeness, which is the meaning of the Latin *salus,* from which our word "salvation" comes. We have stated that Jesus Christ is concerned that people live in at least four primary right relationships. Now evaluate your church in terms of its concern about these four areas:

1. A right relationship to God, expressed in faith and obedience.

2. A right relationship to oneself in terms of self-understanding and self-acceptance, resulting from a vital experience of the love of God.

3. A right relationship to the significant others with whom we live and work, marked by vulnerability.

4. A right relationship to the world, which involves us in a responsible ministry to and in and with the world.

Evaluate in which one or two of these relationships your church seems to be the most concerned and in which relationship or relationships your church seems the least concerned or aware. This will give you some idea of the growing edge of your church and what God is trying to add to the concerns He has already given.

## Exercise 3. Style of Life

Let's now consider something of a style of life in your church. A friend of ours, an Air Force colonel, headed up a base in England just after World War II. He was fond of asking the question, "What is the uniform of a Christian?" He was really asking, "What is different about the style of life of a Christian?" In other words, how do members of a church relate to one another and to the world in a way that is different, and that is a witness to the indwelling Christ?

How would you characterize the life-style evidenced by your church membership?

1. Do the members of your church tend to lead from strength or to lead from weakness?

2. Are the members of your church, by and large, involved in relevant ways in the needs of persons and situations in your community?

3. Is your church run by dynamic individuals, or by group and team effort?

4. In the pulpit and in the pew do you find non-theoretical, experiential language used, or technical, theological language?

5. Does your church apply pressure for people to join, or is there freedom for a new person coming into your midst?

6. Does your church pray for the courage to make costly changes "beginning with me" whenever necessary?

7. Does the church say to the non-churched people in your town, "Come and be like us," or does it say, "We are like you"?

8. Does your church attempt to discover Christ *with* people, or to bring Christ *to* people?

## Exercise 4

Here is an interesting evaluation, recently used as a guide-line for a denomination. It has to do with whether your church is healthy as an institution.

| *An Unhealthy Institution.* | *A Healthy Institution.* |
|---|---|
| 1. Institutional response to crises. | Institutional response to goals. |
| 2. Unclear goals. | Clear goals (even if they are wrong). |
| 3. Strategy designated by special interest. | Strategy outgrowth of group process. |
| 4. Communication: noisy and mistrustful. | Communication: clear and trustworthy. |
| 5. Appraisal by folk wisdom. | Appraisal by precept standards. |
| 6. Resistance to change. | Openness to change. |
| 7. Finances unclear except to leaders. | Financial condition understood. |
| 8. Personnel diverse and unacceptable to one another. | Personnel complementary and team-oriented. |
| 9. Conflicts over roles and responsibilities. | Roles and responsibilities clearly defined. |
| 10. Authority and responsibility separated. | Authority and responsibility united. |
| 11. Members overworked or underworked. | Members with a reasonable work load. |

*Suggested Reading List*

Bonhoeffer, Dietrich
    The Cost of Discipleship          Macmillan
    Life Together                  Harper & Row
Casteel, John L. (Ed.)
    The Creative Role of Interpersonal
        Groups in the Church      Association Press
    Spiritual Renewal through Personal
        Groups               Association Press
Coleman, Lyman
    Acts Alive                Christian Outreach
    Groups Alive (and other study guides)  Christian Outreach
Cox, Harvey
    Feast of Fools            Harvard University
                            Press
    God's Revolution and Man's
        Responsibility          Judson
    The Secular City          Macmillan
    The Church Amid Revolution    Association Press
Drakeford, John
    The Awesome Power of the
        Listening Ear          Word
Engquist, Richard (Ed.)
    Is Anyone for Real? (January, 1971)  Word
    Living the Great Adventure     Word
Gilkey, Langdon
    How the Church Can Minister to the
        World without Losing Itself   Harper & Row

Haughton, Rosemary
    The Act of Love                  Lippincott
    On Trying to Be Human    Templegate
    Why Be a Christian?      Lippincott
Howard, Walden
    Nine Roads to Renewal    Word
Howard, Walden (Ed.)
    Groups That Work       Zondervan
Howe, Reuel L.
    The Creative Years      Seabury
    Herein Is Love          Judson
    Man's Need and God's Action   Seabury
    The Miracle of Dialogue   Seabury
    Partners in Preaching    Seabury
Jabay, Earl
    The God Players       Zondervan
    Search for Identity     Zondervan
Johnson, Ben C.
    The Lay Witness Mission   Institute of Church
                                        Renewal
Larson, Bruce
    Dare To Live Now!     Zondervan
    Living on the Growing Edge Zondervan
    Setting Men Free       Zondervan
Miller, Keith
    The Habitation of Dragons  Word
    A Second Touch          Word
    The Taste of New Wine    Word
Milliken, William E.
    Tough Love            Revell
Monro, Claxton and Taegel, Wm. S.
    Witnessing Laymen Make
        Living Churches      Word
O'Connor, Elizabeth
    Call to Commitment     Harper & Row
    Journey Inward, Journey Outward  Harper & Row
Ogilvie, Lloyd J.
    A Life Full of Surprises   Abingdon
Olsson, Karl A.
    By One Spirit           Covenant
Osborne, Cecil
    The Art of Understanding Yourself  Zondervan

Pannell, William
    My Friend, the Enemy                  Word
Perry, John D., Jr.
    The Coffee House Ministry        John Knox
Phillips, J. B.
    The Ring of Truth               Macmillan
    Your God Is Too Small          Macmillan
Raines, Robert A.
    New Life in the Church         Harper & Row
    Reshaping the Christian Life    Harper & Row
    The Secular Congregation      Harper & Row
Reid, Clyde
    Groups Alive, Church Alive     Harper & Row
Shoemaker, Samuel M.
    The Experiment of Faith      Harper & Row
    Extraordinary Living for Ordinary Men  Zondervan
    Under New Management       Zondervan
    With the Holy Spirit and with Fire   Word
Steere, Douglas V.
    Dimensions of Prayer         Harper & Row
Stringfellow, William
    Count It All Joy              Eerdmans
    Dissenter in a Great Society    Abingdon
    Free in Obedience           Seabury
    Instead of Death            Seabury
    My People Is the Enemy       Doubleday
    A Private and Public Faith     Eerdmans
Teilhard de Chardin, Pierre
    The Divine Milieu          Harper & Row
    The Future of Man          Harper & Row
    Man's Place in Nature       Harper & Row
    The Phenomenon of Man     Harper & Row
    Science and Christ         Harper & Row
Tournier, Paul
    The Adventure of Living      Harper & Row
    Guilt and Grace            Harper & Row
    The Healing of Persons      Harper & Row
    The Meaning of Persons     Harper & Row
    A Place for You            Harper & Row
    The Seasons of Life        John Knox
    The Strong and the Weak    Westminster
    To Understand Each Other    John Knox

Trueblood, Elton
 Alternative to Futility     Harper & Row
 The Company of the Committed  Harper & Row
 The Humor of Christ     Harper & Row
 The Incendiary Fellowship   Harper & Row
 A Place to Stand      Harper & Row
 The Yoke of Christ      Harper & Row
Verney, Stephen
 Fire in Coventry      Revell
Webber, George W.
 The Congregation in Mission   Abingdon
Whiston, Lionel A.
 Are You Fun To Live With?   Word
Winter, Gibson
 Love and Conflict      Doubleday
 Suburban Captivity of the Churches Macmillan

## RELATED SECULAR BOOKS OF UNUSUAL INTEREST

Fromm, Erich
 The Art of Loving      Harper & Row
Gardner, John W.
 Self-Renewal       Harper & Row
Glasser, William
 Reality Therapy      Harper & Row
Jourard, Sidney
 The Transparent Self    Van Nostrand-
               Reinhold

May, Rollo
 Love and Will       Norton
Mowrer, O. Hobart
 The Crisis in Psychiatry and Religion Van Nostrand-
               Reinhold

 The New Group Therapy    Van Nostrand-
               Reinhold